The Noble Newfoundland Dog

A History in Stories, Legends and the Occasional Tall Tale

Bruce Hynes

NIMBUS PUBLISHING

Nimbus Publishing Limited
PO Box 9166
Halifax, NS   B3K 5M8
(902) 455-4286

Printed and bound in Canada

Design: Margaret Issenman, MGDC

Library and Archives Canada Cataloguing in Publication

       Hynes, Bruce, 1940-
       The noble Newfoundland dog : a history in stories,
       legends and the occasional tall tale / Bruce Hynes.

Includes bibliographical references.
ISBN 1-55109-544-0

1. Newfoundland dog. I. Title.

SF429.N4H95 2005   636.73   C2005-905140-X

We acknowledge the financial support of the Government of Canada through the Book
Publishing Industry Development Program (BPIDP) and the Canada Council, and of the Province
of Nova Scotia through the Department of Tourism, Culture and Heritage for our publishing
activities.

Dedicated to all the
Newfoundland dogs
whose deeds and suffering
have gone
unrecognized and unrecorded.

Preface

This book is an amalgamation of history, anecdotes, and personal experiences compiled by a devotee of Newfoundland dogs. The popular breed has for centuries prompted writers to record stories about its heroism, loyalty, and intelligence, and I have included here tales from many different sources. I have credited books, magazines, websites, and television shows, but the origins of the many stories that have come to me by word of mouth from other Newfoundland enthusiasts must remain a mystery.

Many of these stories may seem unbelievable, and, while I cannot vouch for the truthfulness of those who presented some of the tales or those who repeated them, I find them all fascinating and hope you will, too.

Kennel names, when known, are in parentheses on the first occurrence. The owner of a kennel usually selects a name, such as "Westerland Kennels," "Little Bear Kennels," "Gypsy," etc. Puppies are then named with the kennel's name as a prefix, such as "Westerland Knight" or "Gypsy Baron." The abbreviation Ch., for champion, indicates that a dog has garnered a specific number of points at dog shows. This qualification is important in breeding and in determining the quality of a dog's lineage.

Terms marked with an asterisk in this book are defined in the glossary.

One last, very important, point: My dogs are not Newfoundlanders, but Newfoundlands. I, their owner, am a Newfoundlander.

Contents

Introduction

To describe the dog as "man's best friend" may be a tiresome cliché, but its perpetual use is grounded in truth. It's out of the question to attempt to include in any book the inestimable obligation humanity has to the dog, or even to one breed of dog. Further, I assert that dogs' devotion and service derive not from a submissive or timid nature, but from a sense of affinity and a high intelligence which is, in some ways, superior to our own.

In the mid-nineteenth century, Henry Hawkes of Halling, Kent, founder of music and musical instrument producer Hawkes and Company, wrote:

> In man, true friendship I long strove to find,
> but missed my aim;
> At length I found it in my dog most kind.
> Man! blush for shame.

The large, sturdy Newfoundland is perhaps one of the very best canine friends people have been lucky enough to have. It is known for its intelligence, gentle disposition, and centuries of service rescuing those in peril, particularly anyone in danger of drowning. The breed is the most versatile of working dogs. Their disposition and gentle nature shine through in therapy work, they excel as trackers and draught animals, and they are discriminating guard dogs and capital babysitters. Their beauty and brawn have made them successful competitors in the show ring as well as in trials of obedience, draughting, and water activities.

Tales of the Newfoundland dog—of its heroism, of its under-standing, faithfulness, general intelligence, endurance, and sense of humour—could fill volumes. There have been many stories told and written of other breeds, but never has there been a dog that has so consistently fostered stories such as those of the Newfoundland. Considering the scarcity of the dogs, it's astonishing that they are so well known and admired. If only half the reports are true, the Newfoundland must be a truly remarkable creature.

Newfoundlands seem to consider their *raison d'être* to be keep-ing people from harm. Their heroic rescues, searches, and acts of selflessness are legendary. All the same, the acts that endear them to their owners and fans are those you seldom hear of. A small child is stopped at the end of the driveway, a stranger warned away from the door, a homeowner is alerted with a late-night *woof* to the smell of smoke, or a lost and frightened child is put at ease.

Many dogs affect their owners' lives in positive and heartwarm-ing ways. But this dog has the sometimes eerie ability to read its companions' moods and try to help. It's always nearby if someone's ill, and one can't help but feel better for its tranquil presence. It shows concern if you're emotionally or physically hurt, it will lis-ten as long as necessary without showing annoyance, and it never offers unwelcome advice. Have an unpleasant dispute and even if you're wrong, it still considers you the greatest person in the world. Come home after a bad day and it seems brighter because that Newfoundland is waiting, tail wagging and with a slipper in his mouth.

Chapter 1

The Newfoundland Dog

Newfoundlands are large dogs, the average weight for a male being 150 pounds, the female 130. They often reach 200 pounds, though some are considerably smaller.

The Newfoundland is one of the few dogs that may be considered indigenous to North America, and has for many years been an outstanding ambassador of its island home. The list of pure-bred Canadian dogs is short: the Nova Scotia duck tolling retriever, the Canadian Eskimo dog, the Tahtlan bear dog (now believed to be extinct), the Labrador retriever, and its close relative, the Newfoundland dog.

A healthy Newfoundland is strong, active, and as much at home in water as on land. Deep bodied, well muscled, and well co-ordinated, the average height for a male is about seventy centimetres, and for a female, sixty-five, though many good specimens are considerably taller or shorter.

A good specimen has an air of lordliness and carries its head proudly, moving freely with a loosely slung body. A slight roll is perceptible when it walks or trots and it does not appear heavy or sluggish.

The Newfoundland's large and dignified head is set on a powerful neck, with a slightly arched crown and a strongly developed occipital bone. Its face is smooth and free of wrinkles, the muzzle clean-cut, square, and fairly short, with well-developed nostrils. The ears lie close to the head, well set back, and are relatively small and triangular, with rounded tips. The soft eyes are dark brown, relatively small, deep-set, and widely spaced. The Newfoundland's expression reflects the character of the breed: benevolent, intelligent, dignified, and of sweet disposition.

Its chest is full and deep and it is broad at the croup with heavily muscled shoulders and very strong loins. The well-muscled hindquarters are perfect for propelling such a big frame through the water or pulling heavy loads. The feet are proportionate to the body, well rounded and tight with firm, arched toes, and are completely webbed. When swimming, the Newfoundland gives the impression of effortless power. The tail is broad and strong at the base and serves as a rudder in the water.

The Newfoundland's double coat is water-resistant. The undercoat is soft and dense, while the outer is moderately long and full (but not shaggy) and lies straight and flat, often with a slight wave. The hair on the head, muzzle, and ears is short and fine, and the legs are feathered all the way down. The tail is covered with long, dense hair, but it does not form a flag.

The dogs are usually black, often with a tinge of bronze or a splash of white on the chest, and sometimes the toes or the

A fine example of the modern-day Newfoundland dog.

tip of the tail are white. There are also some Newfoundlands that are bronze, and one variety, the Landseer, is black-and-white. Landseers arenamed after renowned English painter Sir Edwin Landseer (1802–1873), who frequently painted them.

Probably the most famouse of all Newfoundland dog paintings, Sir Edwin Harry Landseer's *A Distinguished Member of the Humane Society* shows the black-and-white variety of Newfoundland.

The Newfoundland is famous for its disposition. The attitude of the Newfoundland was summed up by Edwin H. Morris of the American Kennel Club in 1925, when he wrote:

> Newfoundlands want to be loved by everyone, particularly by those they know. They respond to approbation, take disapproval intelligently, are quick to learn and remember, and will readily obey. They are not dour or taciturn, but coercion is not liked. While with their friends, a stranger may manifest his individual taste, but a rough word or the slightest act of aggression brings a warning growl, then a show of teeth and on command, they will attack with a ruthless daring. It is fortunate, especially during such lawless periods as present, that these qualities have not been blotted out.
>
> They are comrades of their owners in full sense, or of those they know well, and friendly to strangers when not on guard. They can distinguish between an intruder and a visitor by deportment as well as dress: also, they love children.
>
> —from Morris, *American Kennel Club Gazette*

An excerpt from E. J. Pratt's poem the "Big Fellow" explains the dog's usually placid temperament:

> And I thought of the big Newfoundland
> I saw, asleep by a rock
> The day before,
> That was galvanized by a challenge,
> But eyeing a cur,
> He turned,
> Yawned,
> Closed one eye,
> Then the other,
> And slept.
> —from Pratt, *Here the Tides Flow*

The late Honourable Harold MacPherson (1885–1963), a kennel owner and one of the people responsible for the existence of the breed today, writes:

> Of all the large breeds of dog, none possesses a kindlier or more pleasant disposition and countenance, nor is a more trustworthy and discriminating guardian for children and home, than the Newfoundland....No breed of dogs has greater claim to the title Friend of Man. It is famous for its ability and known readiness to save persons in danger. It is an ideal companion and guard, a discriminating watchdog. If made a member of the family he will defend his master, growl if another person speaks roughly, and in no case of danger will he leave him...The Newfoundland is capable of being trained

for all purposes for which almost every other variety of dog is used, and if properly cared for, and associated with they seem to want only the faculty of speech.

—from MacPherson, *The Book of Newfoundland*

Newfoundlands are indeed sensitive, loyal, and trustworthy. They developed into what they are by sharing the family's work and thus spent most of their waking hours with that family. They thrive on companionship and they want to be where their master is, and seem to have been born to work.

Newfoundlands make ideal companions for both adults and children. The big dogs are as amiable as their appearance implies. The endearing Newfoundland disposition, even temperament, great dignity, and devotion to owner and family has made the dog a legend.

Small children will poke a Newfoundland's eyes, pull its ears, climb upon it, and attempt to ride it, but teasing, prodding, and jabbing will bother the dogs not at all. Gently playful, they have been seen entertaining a small child for hours, bearing any indignity with a doggy smile.

Breeders try to maintain the disposition for which the dog has become famous.

Newfoundlands will seldom instigate a fight and are friendly with nearly everything and everyone. They enjoy the companionship of smaller dogs and cats, and many owners keep, in effect, a pet for their dog—an animal to keep the Newfoundland happy and in good company.

Still, Newfoundlands will stand up to a dog or any other creature if need be. Their protective instinct can surface in many ways, and it is common for a Newfoundland to stand between its owner and a stranger. The big dogs seem to realize that their presence serves as a warning, and they have an innate ability to perceive danger to others.

Despite these inarguable traits of the Newfoundland, there have been some detractors of the breed throughout history. Amadeus Anspach, an Anglican minister, came to Newfoundland in 1799 as headmaster of a grammar school in St. John's. In 1802 he was appointed a missionary of the Society for the Propagation of the Gospel in Harbour Grace and Carbonear. He returned to England in 1812 and, in 1819, produced *A History of the Island of Newfoundland*. In it, he mentions the Newfoundland dog.

He didn't quite believe the mawkish tales he'd heard respecting the breed's timid temperament. He owned Jowler*, a Newfoundland, who did not show any sign of a fearful disposition and, besides having a combative tendency, was likewise "fond of poultry of the larger kind." Anspach stated darkly that when Jowler wanted a drink, "Nothing is equal in his estimation to the blood of a sheep."

Naturally, when a dog is loosed for the summer and left unfed (as we shall discover the Newfoundland often was), it has to take care of itself, and out of desperation may hunt. But, we surmise that Jowler was a ranty, degenerate member of the species—or perhaps Anspach should have taken better care of his dog and fed him.

This seeming appreciation of mutton is probably better explained by Joseph Hatton and Reverend Moses Harvey in 1883:

> There are few fine specimens of the world-renowned "Newfoundland dog" to be met with now in the island from

which it derived its name. The common dogs are a wretched mongrel race, cowardly, thievish, and addicted to sheep-killing. By starvation, neglect, and bad treatment the race has degenerated so that few traits of the original remain. The Newfoundland dog thrives better elsewhere, though there are still some superior specimens to be met with in the country.

—from Hatton and Harvey,
Newfoundland, the Oldest British Colony

Chapter 2

Where Did They Come From?

I see no use in not confessing
To trace your breed would keep me guessing;
It would indeed an expert puzzle
To match such legs with jet-black muzzle.
To make a mongrel, as you know,
It takes some fifty types or so,
And nothing in your height or length,
Could make me see how any strain
Could come from mastiff, bull, or Dane.
　　　　—from "Carlo" in Pratt, *Here the Tides Flow*

Although we can consider the Newfoundland one of the few dogs indigenous to North America, its exact origins, as Edwin J. Pratt describes, are indeed a mystery. Strangely, those who write of dogs and dog things have shed little light on the Newfoundland's line of descent—despite years of study, guessing, debate, and outright argument. We aficionados of the dog have always been curious about the ancestors of our worthy friend and are interested in knowing what bloodlines produced the specimens we have. Somehow the intellect, courage, docility, love of water and retrieving, devotion to children, and unquestioning fidelity that make up the traditional Newfoundland have been maintained.

These traits are all evident in the immediate progenitors of the breed, which are a little more easy to identify than its more distant ancestors. There are four known varieties, all of which undoubtedly mingled with each other and other dogs to contribute to the Newfoundland we know today.

Even up until the 1950s, Newfoundlands were commonly referred to as "water dogs"; this was a nod to the older version of the breed—a big, powerful dog with a straight coat that was either black, brown, tan, or any combination of the three. This dog was also frequently called the great Newfoundland, and is often considered the "true" Newfoundland ancestor, with the closest link to today's Newfoundland dog.

The great Labrador, another large variety, had a more loosely knit frame, and was either wavy or curly coated, with considerable amounts of white in its fur.

The lesser Newfoundland was a smaller, relatively short-haired version, and was also called the lesser St. John's water dog or the smooth-coated retriever. This small variety undoubtedly evolved as the Labrador retriever, which was commonly referred to as such by the 1870s, and, despite titular evidence to the contrary, comes from Newfoundland. There also existed a curly-coated lesser Newfoundland.

Regardless of their shared traits and the popularity of their descendants, just how these four strains developed remains a mystery. Certainly some clues to the Newfoundland's origins exist in its modern-day appearance. The Tibetan mastiff is probably the ancestor of most mastiff breeds and its impressive conformation and size resemble that of the Newfoundland dog greatly.

An 1885 woodcut shows the Tibet dog that so closely resembles the Newfoundland.

The mastiff, however, carries its plumed tail curled over its back—and, more importantly, is noted for its ferocity rather than gentleness. (This trait has probably been enhanced, if not outright encouraged, by training and by its being chained. When raised in a different environment, Tibetan mastiffs are apparently as compliant as most other dogs.)

The Newfoundland also bears a striking resemblance to the dhoghee, an ancient breed of Tibet, Nepal, and Bhutan that has nearly died out and is at least related to the Tibetan mastiff, if not a direct offshoot. There the dhoghee, like the Newfoundland, has been an all-purpose dog—guardian, herder, pack animal and, more notably, the constant companion of children. The Newfoundland closely resembles the Great Pyrenees, but is somewhat larger.

There are three main hypotheses concerning the Newfoundland's ancestry. The first is that it arrived on the island with some of Newfoundland's indigenous people; the second, that it is the result of a cross between dogs brought by the Vikings and the black wolf; and the third, that it is a fortunate amalgam of dogs brought from Europe by early explorers, fishermen, and settlers.

The argument that the Newfoundland is a descendant of a dog belonging to the Beothuk, Newfoundland's indigenous people, continues to crop up, but there is little possibility of it being valid. Many North American tribes had dogs that assisted them in hunting, acted as guardians, or were kept for meat or as sacrificial gifts for the gods, but it has been more or less determined that the Beothuk did not keep dogs.

Without doubt, the ancestor of the Newfoundland was the first domesticated animal on the island, but hard evidence concurs with the reports that no dogs kept company with the Beothuk. No dog remains of any sort have ever been associated with a Beothuk burial.

Physical evidence decrying the notion of Beothuk dogs comes from a 1987 faunal analysis carried out by Dr. Ralph Pastore. Pastore examined animal bones from a Beothuk midden at Boyd's Cove, in Notre Dame Bay, on the Island's northeast coast. None of the bones had been gnawed upon; from this it can be concluded that no dogs were present (or else they were extremely well fed).

John Guy, who was in Newfoundland between 1607 and 1613, had several encounters with the Beothuk and spoke knowledgeably of their way of life, but made no mention of dogs, and English army captain George Cartwright observed in his report on the Beothuk in 1768 that "providence has even denied them the pleasing services and companionship of the faithful dog."

This point was verified by other authorities, namely Lieutenant John Cartwright, RN, George's brother, who discovered Red Indian Lake, and John Peyton Jr., merchant and magistrate of the towns of Exploits and Twillingate.

Captain Cartwright said that, with but one exception, none of the fishermen or trappers with whom he had spoken about the Beothuk mentioned dogs. Peyton was more definite when asked by the English geologist T. G. B. Lloyd about native dogs; he denied there were any. Captain David Buchan, who spent the years between 1818 and 1835 in Newfoundland, was intimate with the Beothuk and he, like

Guy two hundred years before him, neglected to mention dogs of any sort.

There have been voices opposing this view. Jehan Mallart, a Dutchman who cruised along the coast of the island from 1545 to 1547, pointed out that the Native people of Newfoundland were tall, finely shaped men whose diet consisted of fruit, fish, and raw meat. In addition, he reported, they owned dogs. No one knows how he acquired this knowledge, and since we know the Beothuk cooked their food, little credence has been given to Mallart's story. Since then it has been noted by a number of writers that he dispensed the truth with great economy.

In March 1819, a Beothuk woman, Demasduit, was captured by John Peyton Jr. at Red Indian Lake, the headwaters of Newfoundland's largest river, the Exploits. She was called Mary March by her captors. "E. S.," suspected to be one of the Slade merchant family of the Twillingate and Fogo area, was present when she was taken. He described the dogs that he saw: "A bitch and her whelps, about two months old, in one of the Beothuk houses." Since most of E. S.'s details were supported by others, his remarks should not be ignored. But just because someone saw a dog and her pups in one house doesn't mean the Beothuk commonly owned and used dogs. This is the only instance where anyone of repute saw a dog with the Beothuk, and Europeans had been established on the Island for three hundred years.

Megan Nutbeem, among the foremost of Newfoundland breeders and experts, attributed the dog's loyalty, lifesaving skills, and sagacity to the relationship it may have shared with the Beothuk, despite what Cartwright, Peyton, and others had said. In an article written for *The Book of Newfoundland* in 1935, she contends:

The Indians regarded their dogs as gifts from the gods and through this mutual relationship of affection and dependence on each other grew two races—the gentle Indian and the dependable Newfoundland. There is little question that the inherent qualities of our dog were instilled in him by this strong human relationship.

When Shanawdithit, a niece of Demasduit, was taken in 1811, while quite young, by Captain David Buchan of HMS *Grasshopper*, she provided explorer William Epps Cormack with a word list that included the Beothuk term for "dog." Cormack, who continued to explore the interior of Newfoundland until 1830, became familiar with the Beothuk and produced a report in which he made a note: "Whether the Beothuk had any dogs amongst them or domestic animals '(No)'." It appears Shanawdithit gave him this information.

Around 1900 James Lumsden of Newtown, Bonavista Bay, said that the origin of the Newfoundland, though it derived its name from the island, was obscure, and authorities said that: "It is doubtful whether the aborigines had the dog at all; and it is highly improbable that it is indigenous. Some happy crossing of breeds may have produced it here."

Joseph Hatton and naturalist and essayist Reverend Moses Harvey, co-authors of *Newfoundland, the Oldest British Colony*, also doubted that the dog had sprung from the earth of Newfoundland: "The origin of this fine breed is lost in obscurity. It is doubtful whether the aborigines possessed the dog at all."

Is it plausible that a Viking dog had something to do with the Newfoundland? Perhaps, as many have speculated, the latter developed from dogs brought to the New World by Vikings more than a thousand years ago. It is said that Scandinavians had dogs not unlike the Newfoundland, and it may be that a few of these mated with the native wolves on the island, creating a dog with the Scandinavian dog's outstanding physique, courage, and intelligence.

In Norway the large, black, Scandinavian "bear dogs" were used as beasts of burden and as guardians. W. L. C. Martin wrote in *History of the Dog* (1845) that Norwegian peasants had dogs much like Newfoundlands. They outfitted the dogs with spiked collars to fend off wolves attempting to grasp their throats. He further noted, with wonder, that even bears usually retreated before these dogs. If this is so, they most probably had the blood of the Tibetan mastiff or dhoghee running in their veins.

Certainly some of the Viking dogs could have been left behind when their owners departed Newfoundland, and, if not, they could have mingled with North American dogs or wolves during their visit. Left undisturbed for more than five hundred years, the breed could have evolved into a dog that was perfectly suited to a land of cold, snow, ice, rock, stunted trees, and the ever-present sea. The dog would have had to swim to make a living, even if unaccompanied by humans, and the Newfoundland certainly has a liking for fish and fishing.

Disregarding the fact that other Europeans, and possibly Asians, certainly visited the island earlier than the Norse, proponents of this theory have apparently been vindicated in recent years. They gleefully point out that it has been conclusively proven that L'Anse aux

Meadows, at the northern tip of Newfoundland's Great Northern Peninsula, was a Viking colony, likely Leif Ericsson's Vinland. Thus, the theory of the dog's origin has been established with a greater degree of confidence—the Norse sagas state that Ericsson and his Vikings brought their "bear dogs" to Vinland with them.

But perhaps our subject is a dog from Europe, pure and simple. Five hundred years after the departure of the Vikings, other Europeans arrived in Newfoundland. It is said that in 1506 Jean Denys of Honfleur or Harfleur (there's some confusion as to which: both are at the mouth of the Seine in Basque territory), of France established a base in Newfoundland at Rougnoust or Rougnose, now Renews. It is difficult to imagine anyone of that time establishing a base without having the company of a few dogs to warn against attack or to help in the hunt, and we know with certainty that a European dog arrived within a short time.

Beginning in 1612, Richard Whitbourne, later Sir Richard, traded between Newfoundland and Europe. Pirates were a constant hazard and he was appointed by the High Court of Admiralty in 1615 to establish some sort of law on the island. He was then invited to govern Welshman William Vaughn's colony at Renews. He did so from 1618 to 1620, and after his retirement published his memoirs. In them he states that the local "wolves and beasts" came to his fish flakes* and caused a disturbance, and that "each time my mastiffe-dogge went unto them…the one began to fawne and play with the other."

It seems the dog and his new friend went into the woods together for nine or ten days at a time, and the dog always returned unharmed. Since wolves and dogs are natural enemies, it must be reckoned the visitor was another dog. Whitbourne made it clear that the friendship struck him as odd: "Hereof I am in no way superstitious, yet it is something strange to me that the wild beasts, being followed by a sterne Mastiff-dogge, should grow to familiaritie with him, seeing their natures are repugnant." (It should also be noted that mastiff, in the sense used by Whitbourne, does not pertain to the breed we know today as a mastiff, but was a sort of general term used to describe any large guard dog.)

This view was, in particular, held by American Edwin H. Morris in an article for the American Kennel Club (AKC) in 1925, in which he contends that the breed resulted from the mating of local Newfoundland "water dogs" with those dogs introduced by adventurers and European fishing fleets of the seventeenth and eighteenth centuries.

Possibly even prior to John Cabot's rediscovery of Newfoundland in 1497, and certainly subsequent to it, Spanish, French, and Basque fishermen brought the Pyrenean mountain dog or its ancestors with them and they, no doubt, contributed genetic material to the Newfoundland's makeup.

As early as 1662 the French wintered in Newfoundland, particularly at Plaisance, or Placentia, as it is known today. When the Basques and French came to fish, part of their provisions were sheep that could live comfortably off the land. Some believe the Pyrenean dogs were brought to deal with wolves and other animals that might prey on the flocks.

Other possible participants in this amalgam are the Leonberger, St. Bernard, mastiff, and Portuguese water dog. Conversely, according to some authorities, most of these dogs descended, at least in part, from the Newfoundland!

As for the Landseer variety, many experts, including Megan Nutbeem, contend that it evolved sometime between 1550 and 1700 as a result of the mingling of the all-black Newfoundlands with the white "estate dogs" of England, and that after two hundred years of crossbreeding, the type was standardized. Though many agree, there is certainly no concensus—it seems there is too much resistance to the possibility that the original Newfoundland was a black-and-white dog.

If we suppose that Pyrenean dogs brought to Newfoundland were dependable shepherds when their owners were at sea, we must consider their other attributes. They were moderately large, active, faithful, of a dignified mien, with flat coarse coats and woolly undercoats adequate for the harsh climate of the Pyrenees. They also had unfathomable, searching, intelligent eyes, and the deep flews* that lent to good olfactory nerves.

Now, suppose that when the English colonized Newfoundland they brought such sporting dogs as were in vogue in their native land. Probably these were curly-coated retrievers, black dogs of medium size. The dogs had long muzzles, were inclined to be hard headed and hard mouthed, made good dogs for retrieving on land or water, and were alert and intelligent. Possibly the fishermen's Pyrenean dog crossed with that of English sportsmen, and from this evolved the greater Newfoundland water dog, probably black-and-white—the progenitor of the Newfoundland

An etching entitled *The Newfoundland Dog—Original Breed*, showing the dog as it appeared in the 1700s according to Macgillivray's *History of British Quadrupeds*.

we know today. Then, we must also consider the white spot on the chest of female black wolves the origin of the same marking on Newfoundlands today. Of course, Spaniards brought dogs too, as did the Portuguese, Dutch, and Channel Islanders, and these likely contributed to the breed to some degree.

There is little doubt that the breed derived from "native dogs"— that is, a mixture of black wolves, Algonquian dogs, Viking dogs, and those brought by Europeans when they came to fish Newfoundland waters in the fifteenth century.

Of course all matters can be resolved if the government takes an interest. When the Newfoundland dog was made the province's official animal in 1972, the executive council's proclamation of October 5 ordered that an account of the dog's origin, right or wrong, be standardized, and, right or wrong, that must settle it:

> The Newfoundland dog is indigenous to the island of Newfoundland. Documented proof shows that in 3000 BC the Maritime Archaic Indians in Newfoundland buried their dogs with their dead. It is also recorded that the Beothuk and Mountaineer Indians, who inhabited Newfoundland before the white man, used native dogs as companions, guardians and beasts of burden.

> When Leif Ericsson visited Newfoundland in 1001 AD, he carried with him both family and animals. These big black bear dogs mated with and re-invigorated the native Newfoundland dogs. For another four hundred years, there were no visitors to the shores of this island home, and by the time European

fishermen started to arrive in the early sixteenth century, there was established a very definite breed of Newfoundland dog.

By the time colonization was allowed in Newfoundland in 1610, the distinct physical characteristics and mental attributes had been established in the Newfoundland for all time.

It is interesting to note that the earliest known dogs in Newfoundland were not as large as those of the present day. A larger and heavier dog became evident after the Viking expedition and size increased once again when the white man arrived. The increase in size occurred not only from the infusion of foreign bloodlines, but as naturally as man's size increased. The Newfoundland is a natural pure-bred, and has developed because his natural geographical situation and the demands of his environment shaped him to be what he is and what he does.

Had the government taken a firm stand earlier, we may have avoided the confusion and arguments about the origin of the Newfoundland dog that have prevailed for the past few hundred years.

Chapter 3

Disaster and Resurgence

George Cartwright supposedly named the Newfoundland when in his diary, dated January 1771, he referred to "Mr. Jones' faithful Newfoundland dog." This is the earliest recorded reference to a Newfoundland dog by that name.

Unfortunately, the newly minted Newfoundland dog was under serious threat just nine years later. Newfoundland governor Captain Richard Edwards, RN, appointed in 1757, is best remembered for trying to reduce the number of dogs in Newfoundland. (Edwards is often confused with his predecessor, another Captain Richard Edwards—of no relation—who was governor from 1746 to 1757.) The second Governor Edwards attempted to advance sheep breeding in 1780, to build an island industry that would provide wool for English mills. To facilitate such an industry he decreed that no family could have more than one dog; this was supposed to reduce the loss of sheep to predators, often assumed to by roaming, hungry dogs.

At this time the future of the Newfoundland breed was by no means a sure thing; in fact, it was beginning to look very shaky. Reverend Charles Pedley writes:

> One of the native productions for which Newfoundland is famous in other countries is its dogs. But from a proclamation by Governor Edwards in 1780 it appears that either there was

then manifest that corruption of the breed which is so plain to visitors who look on the canine varieties which abound in St. John's at this day, or that their beauty was more than counterbalanced by their noxiousness, which also is a very common complaint at the present time. The following is the text of the proclamation.

Whereas it has been represented to me that the number of dogs kept by merchants, boatkeepers, and others in this town is become a very great nuisance and injury to the inhabitants, I do therefore hereby give notice that if, after the 31st day of August, any merchant, boatkeeper, or others shall be legally convicted of keeping more than one dog, he or they so offending shall pay a fine of twenty shillings for every dog above one kept by him or them; and I do hereby authorise any and every person to kill all the dogs above one known to be kept by any merchant, boatkeeper, or others as aforesaid.

—from Pedley, *History of Newfoundland*

For most breeds on the island this decision was not as detrimental, since there were others of their type scattered around the world. For the Newfoundland it nearly meant extinction, as they were few and were found only on the island. The dog population diminished significantly, but the vaunted sheep farming industry was a failure for some reason (as are most government incursions into commerce) and the dogs slowly rebounded.

Edwards was followed as governor by Admiral John Campbell in 1782, and he allowed the dogs to be taken to England by anyone who wished to take them. According to *The Recollections of James Anthony*

Gardner, some seventy dogs were taken on one ship alone. This was good news for the breed; some of the original Newfoundlands were preserved, and many were judiciously mixed with other dogs in hopes of improving the breed.

Governor Admiral William Waldegrave (who served from 1797 to 1800) is generally seen as having had a genuine interest in the welfare of Newfoundland. Nevertheless, he spent his winters in London and in 1798 was seemingly unaffected by the news of near mutiny at Fort William, near the town of St. John's. To keep the soldiers, who were virtually starving, under control he decided to strike a blow against their pastimes. He forbade them visits to bawdy houses and grog shops and banned the adoption of pets. The custom of soldiers adopting animals, in particular dogs, was one of the most innocuous, but he ordered all dogs found near the fort after the sunset gun bayoneted or hung.

The intellectual anaemia that earlier afflicted governors now infected the Court of Sessions at St. John's. Chief Justice Caesar Colclough struck another blow against the Newfoundland in February 1815 when, despite the value of dogs to the local economy, he ordered that all dogs—Newfoundland or otherwise—found at large in or around the city be destroyed. To help things along, a bounty of five shillings was paid for each dog killed. Since most dogs were allowed to roam during the off-season this, once more, meant the virtual demise of the Newfoundland dog on the island.

In areas where enforcement was lax, in the outports and on the west coast, these dictates were usually ignored. However, in the St. John's region the dogs all but disappeared.

The killing of dogs aroused such indignation among the settlers that some risked all to protect their animals. A letter was fastened to the Court House gate:

To the Honorable Cesar Colclough, Esq., Chief Judge in the Supreme Court of St. John's and in and over the Island of Newfoundland, &c., &c., &c.

The humble petition of the distressd of St. John's in general must humbly sheweth:—

That the poor of St. John's are very much oppressed by different orders from the Court House, which they amigine is unknown to your Lordship, Concerning the killing and shooting of their doggs, without the least sine of the being sick or mad. We do hope that your Lordship will check the Justices that was the means of this eveil Proclamation agianst the Interest of the poor Families, that their dependence for their Winter's Fewel is on their Doggs, and likewise several single men that is bringing out Wood for the use of the Fishery, if in case this business is not put back it will be the means of an indeferent business as ever the killing of the Doggs in Ireland was before the rebellion the first Instance will be given by Killing Cows and Horses, and all other disorderly Vice that can be comprehened by the Art of Man.

We are sorry for giveing your Lordship any uneasines for directing any like business to your Honour, but Timely notice is better than use any voilance. What may be the cause of what we not wish to ment at present, by puting a stop to this great evil. We hope thay our Prayrs will be mains of obtaining Life Everlasting for your Lordship in the world to come.

Mercy wee will take, and Mercy wee will give.
      —from Prowse, *A History of Newfoundland*

The terrified Colclough immediately put forth a proclamation offering a reward of one hundred pounds for the identity of the writer or the person who posted it. He had no takers and shortly afterward retired and returned to Ireland.

Geologist Joseph Beete Jukes indicates in an 1842 book that the breed was becoming very scarce in Newfoundland:

> The day before we left I bought a good dog from one of the Indians [Mi'kmaq] for ten shillings. Newfoundland is one of the worst places in the world for getting a good, or at least a good-looking Newfoundland dog. In St. John's and its neighbourhood they are the most ill-looking set of mongrels that can be conceived. In the more distant ports, however, the breed has been better preserved.
> —from Jukes, *Excursions in and About Newfoundland*

The vendetta against the Newfoundland was begun anew in 1860, when legislation was again passed to protect sheep and other domestic animals against dogs. Each dog was to be clogged*, and if it was found otherwise, without its owner, it was to be destroyed.

A c.1885 woodcut by German artist W. Sperling, entitled *Neufundlaender*, shows a typical Newfoundland dog at the time of the second anti-dog act.

Despite the fact that at the Westminster Kennel Club (WKC) show in 1877 there were twelve Newfoundlands in competition, and despite the recognition of the breed and its potential value (much greater than that of Newfoundland sheep), another act was passed in 1884.

Now the clogs had to bear the owner's name and any dogs—other than pointers, spaniels, and terriers licensed by the magistrate—without a name on their clogs could be shot by anyone.

In 1890, the persistent issue of sheep farming cropped up afresh in Newfoundland and, in response, Chapter 141 of the *Consolidated Statutes* of 1892 outlined legislation governing the ownership of dogs. The government, in effect, decided to kill off all but sheep dogs to prevent predation. (This was another half-witted move; there were virtually no sheep dogs in Newfoundland and very few sheep.) The 1500 to 2500 Newfoundland dogs on the island once more faced extinction.

Ironically, modern day Newfoundlands in Australia have been trained to be excellent sheepdogs—not herders in particular, but protectors.

Even though the Newfoundland went through brutal times on its own island, outsiders recognized the value of the breed. In 1815, midshipman Sidney Smith of HMS *Drake* was assigned to the crew of its cutter, which John Peyton Jr. was to pilot into and around Notre Dame Bay and up the Exploits River on Newfoundland's northeast coast. Smith was impressed by the grandeur of the river and also took a keen interest in the Newfoundland breed that Peyton kept as working dogs.

After Smith left the Exploits area to return to St. John's in July, Peyton's Newfoundland bitch produced a litter. When the puppies were a few weeks old two of them were sent to St. John's, one for Smith and one for Chief Justice Francis Forbes, and they were very well received.

Many years later Smith, now a captain, wrote a letter to Peyton, dated October 18 1850, that states in part:

You sent after me to St. John's a puppy of your breed (in conjunction with one for Chief Justice Forbes). My dog was eventually carried by my father to Caen in Normandy where they both died of old age, the dog first. His body was begged by the public museum as the finest specimen of his variety the French had ever seen. He was stuffed and is at this moment a conspicuous ornament in the gallery of Natural History, Hotel de Ville, Caen…
    —from Peyton, *River Lords*

Available references indicate that he resides there to this day!

The following paragraph appeared in *The Labrador Dog* at around the same time as the above quotation:

In Australia the Newfoundland dog thrives vigorously. Colonel Mundy, who served there as Deputy Adjutant-General, has left an account of his experiences, and he writes in 1846: "Some of the Newfoundland dogs in this country are the finest I have ever seen—much larger and handsomer than the Labrador dog, which is neither very tall nor curly in the coat."
    —from George and Middleton, *The Labrador Dog*

By 1808, Lord Byron had granted his dog, Boatswain, immortality in his poetry, and around the mid-1850s, Massachusetts naturalist, philosopher, and author Henry David Thoreau also mentioned the Newfoundland dog: "A man is not a good man to me because he will feed me if I should be starving or pull me out of a ditch if I should ever fall into one. I can find a Newfoundland that will do as much and more." (From *Encyclopedia of Newfoundland and Labrador*.)

The British Royal Family likewise owned Newfoundland dogs and, according to legend, one who saved the life of his unidentified royal master lies buried in the grounds of Windsor Castle.

The dogs' charm and intelligence quickly captivated the English and the demand for them was far in excess of the supply. When his grandson was born, Sir Walter Scott wrote that he hoped his dog Mungo approved of the newcomer, and later he gave his grandson a fitting gift: a Newfoundland puppy. He also wrote a tribute to the Newfoundland dog that appeared in *British Field Sports*:

> One of the most blameless and good-natured of animals, neither the natural nor intentional enemy of any other. On the contrary, instinctively and voluntarily the friend of all, seeking every occasion to assist and oblige, and in his attachment to human nature equal even to the Spaniel, and inferior to him only in the qualifications of a courtier. To finish the strictly well-merited eulogy of this wonderful brute, where are we, whether among bipeds or quadrupeds, to find his superior for kindness of heart, susceptibility of courage, fortitude and perseverance!
>
> —quoted in MacPherson, *The Book of Newfoundland*

(Unfortunately, at one time Scott also mentioned that he thought perhaps the bear had contributed to the Newfoundland's genetic makeup, but all this proves is that he was no biologist.)

Other developments occurred to help the breed. In 1885 white, black-and-white, and some all-black dogs were sent from

Newfoundland to the North American mainland. In 1886 a specialty club for the Newfoundland was organized and a breed standard drawn up that, with minor revisions, is still in use today. The breed was among the first to be registered in Canada, and the Canadian Kennel Club (CKC) Stud Book lists seven Newfoundlands registered in 1888–1889.

There were still some around Newfoundland, principally on the west coast. Geologist and author James P. Howley, having been appointed to the Geological and Topographical Survey of Newfoundland, spent much time travelling about the island. On June 28, 1889, he spent the night at Sandy Point, near what is now Stephenville, in a big house made available to him by Roman Catholic priest Father Brown. Howley and his dog Flockko took up residence, but while Brown was not home, his "great black dog" Dhu was. Although quite friendly toward Howley, Dhu nearly killed poor Flockko, who had to be sent to stay with the survey crew.

As the Newfoundland found itself in other parts of the world, so it also made its way to Labrador and Quebec where, for the most part, it was not known as a Newfoundland. The dogs were described with a variety of names, often just plain "dog."

Despite all the help the breed obtained from fans far and wide, Harold MacPherson, a Newfoundlander, is probably the most important person in the history of the Newfoundland dog. With the help of his allies in England, Canada, and the United States, MacPherson, on his Westerland Farm at St.

A postcard from the 1920s depicting three of Harold MacPherson's Westerland puppies.

John's, undertook to revive the breed near the beginning of the twentieth century. He was instrumental in saving the breed from oblivion.

He began with a first-rate bitch pup, Guess, a gift from a Captain Hardy (who lived on the west coast of the island, where the dogs had fared somewhat better), and Jack, a very good dog owned by MacPherson's brother, Dr. Cluney MacPherson (inventor of the gas mask in World War One). This was the start of the resurgence. The first dog of this breeding was the rather small but handsome Oscar.

Most of the best dogs were in England, and Earl Grey, Governor General of Canada from 1904 to 1911, sent Bobs, a superb dog from the English kennels, to Dr. Wilfred Grenfell in Labrador as a gift in 1910. The dog arrived too late in the year to catch the northbound steamer for Labrador, and MacPherson agreed to have a friend care for Bobs until delivery was possible. He bred the dog with some of his own and thus introduced sorely needed new blood to the island's Newfoundland stock.

St. John's businessman Eric A. Bowring of the Bowring Brothers' empire further helped revitalize the breed in 1913 by bringing back two descendants of the original stock from England: a dog, Drake (Kayle), and a bitch, Nan (Native Girl). The breed owes much to these dogs and those belonging to MacPherson, who also bred Bowring's dogs with his own.

The resultant offspring were shipped to potential breeders all over the world and MacPherson became the authority on Newfoundlands. 1908 was a turning point for the breed; at the famous Cruft's Show in London, Ch. Shelton Viking, a beautiful Newfoundland, won best in show, all breeds. This spurred some concerted action in England concerning perpetuation of the breed and its purity through a newly formed Newfoundland dog club.

Tragically, during World War One, someone poisoned some of the best specimens, which were in Eleanor Goodall's kennel in England. The criminal reportedly thought the dogs were eating food needed for soldiers. Presumably, this crackpot was also responsible for Goodall's death, for she died soon afterwards, some said from grief.

Goodall used the "Gypsy" prefix and Baron (Ch. Gypsy Baron) was one of her best. Now that the Gypsy strain had been practically wiped out, and as few large dogs were raised in England during the war, those in the British Isles were inbred to an uncomfortable degree.

With the best of England's dogs dead, it was recognized that the breed was in as desperate straits as ever it was. Only one Newfoundland was entered in the New York dog show of 1922, and that one in the miscellaneous class (the infrequency of the breed in shows did not warrant a separate category). Other admirers of the breed, who knew its sterling merit, decided to make the most of those remaining and to reawaken interest in them. They formed the North American Newfoundland Club, and from these modest strata there arose an organization for the welfare of the breed the like of which had never before existed. Harold MacPherson was vice-president of the club in Newfoundland for some years.

The new club adopted a standard of perfection and a points system to reflect it, with specified penalties for defects. Also, at the 1924 Westminster show, the club gave the largest special prize in gold offered for any breed, besides nearly $250 in cash and other specials in five classes.

It was decided in 1925 that those Newfoundlands kept true to type by a few devotees in North America had to be relied upon to revive the breed. Among these were Ch. Chieftain, imported from England by the president of the club, Doctor M. J. Fenton, and others of Shelton Viking stock acquired by Edwin Morris just before the outbreak of World War One.

The future of the breed was by no means certain, and a piece written by A. B. Perlin in 1935, included in *The Book of Newfoundland,* states: "No finer breed of dogs exist, and it is sad to relate that but few thoroughbreds remain in the Island, although efforts are being made to keep the species alive. A thoroughbred pup fetches as much as $100 in Newfoundland today."

One dog stands out above the rest in the attempt to strengthen the gene pool of the North American dogs: the English Siki, famed as the "father of champions." He was a fifth-generation descendant of Shelton Viking, the 1908 show winner, and the Siki line more than any other laid the foundation for most of the successful breeding programmes in the United States and Canada. Though not a spectacular specimen, Siki was nonetheless one of the most prepotent sires in the history of the breed, producing offspring of extraordinary quality. His progeny, brought to the United States in the 1930s, swept the American dogs in competition, and most kennels today can trace their lines back to this all-important Siki bloodline.

These prototypical dogs should not be forgotten. They were the antecedents of the best we have today and deserve a place of honour in the Newfoundland dog hall of fame. Among them were Sir Arthur (Ch. Sir Arthur of Fearless Foundation), Prince (Ch. Prince of Norfolk), and some of the Humber Snowflake stock. Breeder J. Mathieson Rankine mingled Humber Snowflake descendants, his own Lady Hilda, and such noted dogs as Omega, Alpha, Shelton

Viking, Shelton Madge, and Fearless Emblem to produce a number of champions. From them arose Lady Beckey, dam of Ch. Rolfe. Another was the dam of Tip, owned by J. H. Clark, the club's treasurer, who also used his imported dog, Captain.

Sir Arthur and Lady Hilda were imported by Rankine when young, not only for their bloodlines but because their direct ancestors had been subjected to what was considered suitable association with humans. Raising the dogs on Rankine's estate under similar conditions had the desired effect. When a little girl came to visit, she made friends with the dogs, then wandered away across the fields for a walk. When she tired she lay down in the grass beneath a tree and fell asleep. Eventually she was missed and a search was made; she was found using Lady Hilda as a pillow, with Sir Arthur standing vigilant guard. Not until the child was awakened and standing up did Rankine dare approach her.

Another authority and breeder, certainly not to be neglected, is Margaret Booth Chern. She and her husband Vadim owned the famed Little Bear Kennels, a farm high up on the Northfield Mountains in Waitsfield Pass, Vermont. Their contributions to the perpetuation of the Newfoundland breed, maintenance of its standards, and the knowledge they gained and passed on cannot be overestimated. Booth Chern's book, *The New Complete Newfoundland* (1975), is an invaluable reference, and is unfortunately out of print. Because the book is difficult to obtain, a number of its best stories about Newfoundlands are retold here.

Finally, from 1952, Megan Nutbeem and her late husband Robert, both of Newfoundland, were among the leading authorities and breeders with their Harbourbeem Kennels. Megan remains an expert on the breed. In 1974 she became the youngest CKC all-breed judge and has since travelled extensively, judging dogs around the world.

As we should not forget the great dogs of the past, neither should we forget those people responsible for ensuring that the Newfoundland survived as the paragon of dogs that we have to-day.

Chapter 4

A Legend

Much has been said and written of the heroism and intelligence of Newfoundland dogs. They are ever alert and willing to help when danger threatens, but some of these accounts may be apocryphal, and others outright whoppers. Nevertheless, if the owners and acquaintances of these dogs take such pains in bragging of them, there must be a kernel of truth somewhere.

Most of the stories presented here are well documented, ranging from tales of the supernatural to those of heroism, and include several popular yarns that may or may not be myths.

Not surprisingly, big black dogs have established a firm place in the gloomy world of Newfoundland superstitions. Folklorist P. J. Kinsella noted a personal experience in his booklet dealing with such notions:

> The "crying" of a dog foretells death to someone in that neighbourhood, and I myself know of a case where exactly one week before a neighbour died a big Newfoundland dog (and a stranger to the place) came and lay quite docile on the family doorstep for the whole period. At night the animal would "cry" quite pitifully. Shortly after the death of the man, the dog disappeared from the house and vicinity.
> —from Kinsella,
> *Some Superstitions and Traditions of Newfoundland*

Where the dog came from and where it went has never been explained, but this particular belief prevailed among much of the Island's population as late as the 1950s.

Frank Galgay and Michael McCarthy recount in their book *Buried Treasure of Newfoundland and Labrador* that there are rumours of a ghost dog at Aquaforte, a cove familiar to many pirate captains. Aquaforte was settled around 1670 and lies only three miles from Ferryland, which was established some fifty years earlier. Legend has it that around the time of the arrival of the first inhabitants to Aquaforte, a pirate ship was pursued into the community's inner harbour by the Royal Navy. While attempting to elude the man-of-war, the pirates' vessel went aground, and the pirate captain ordered that their ill-gotten gains be taken ashore in the ship's boat. Before leaving the ship, the captain laid a fuse to its magazine, and while he was being rowed to shore the ship exploded, killing the rest of the crew. Evidently, seconds before it went up, the ship's dog leapt over the side and made his way to shore as well. The captain and his boatmen supposedly buried a treasure, then the captain killed them as well.

It was not until many years later the first ghost story surfaced. As an old fisherman prepared for bed one summer night he put his light out, then took a look out his kitchen window to see what weather he might expect the next day. A path leading to the shore ran by his small house of wind-worried clapboard, and he thought he saw two lights approaching along it. He waited and wondered— who would be on the track so late at night? The lights came nearer and he discerned a sound, not unlike the rattle of chains, and he could make out a group of men led by a great black dog with glowing eyes.

It would be easy to find this big black dog terrifying in the middle of the night.

As he watched, he was suddenly frozen with dread and horror. The six men following the dog were shackled and headless. They trudged on down to the shore where the dog walked into the water, followed by the men, and disappeared beneath the surface. As the frightened man stared, a ship rose from the depths of the harbour and, under full sail, made for the open sea with the dog watching from the quarterdeck.

Since then other residents have reported the denizens of the inner harbour and firmly believe the ghosts are the men who rowed the greedy pirate captain to shore. As far as anyone knows, no treasure has ever been recovered.

Another story of treasure recounted by Galgay and McCarthy takes place in Torbay, one of Newfoundland's oldest communities. Torbay was inhabited by three families comprising eighteen people in 1697, when it was destroyed by the French and their Mi'kmaw allies. Migratory fishermen summered there and ships from many countries fished in the harbour. Pirates—infamous thugs such as Peter Easton and William Kidd and a multitude of lesser-known thieves, like Wollaston and Mainwaring for example—often sought refuge there, and buccaneer John Nutt was there as early as 1620. These pirates often went ashore to take on water and sometimes added a fisherman or two to their crew, whether they wanted to join or not.

As usual, the presence of pirates gave rise to tales of treasure buried in the dark of the moon with a dead crewman or hostage left to stand guard. Although there is no conclusive proof that such a thing was done at Treasure Cove, on the north side of Torbay harbour, the story persists.

The tale supposedly came to light when two fishermen from Torbay were returning home after a day's work and put in there. Stepping from their boat, they were met by a huge Newfoundland dog emerging from the woods. They assumed it was from a nearby settlement until they saw its terrible glaring eyes (shades of the Aquaforte ghost dog!). Then, to their consternation, a headless boy bound in chains appeared, following the dog.

The terrified fishermen struggled to float their loaded boat, and despite the ebbing tide that impeded their progress, the encouragement lent by the approaching duo led to an accelerated launching. They scrambled in and, with oars madly flailing in the water, took their leave.

Upon arriving home they told their dreadful tale, and an old man there related a story he had heard from his grandfather as a child. It seems a pirate had taken a Spanish galleon with its cargo of gold and jewels and was searching for a place to hide his plunder until he returned to Europe. Having put in at Torbay he chose a cove and asked for a volunteer to accompany him to the site. The experienced crew knew the volunteer might not return, but a naive youngster, taken from another vessel to act as cabin boy, volunteered.

The boy had befriended the captain's Newfoundland and when they went ashore the dog went with them. After digging a suitable hole at the edge of the woods they set the loot in it, whereupon the captain beheaded the boy with a single stroke of his sword and let his body fall on top of the treasure. This infuriated the dog, who sprang at the captain only to die as well, and his body was thrown in on top of the boy's.

The fishermen who first encountered the singular custodians of the treasure never got over the shock. Shortly afterwards one of them became an invalid, and the other died the same year. Since then there have been other reports of run-ins, of fishermen seeing a headless form walking the beach of Treasure Cove accompanied by a Newfoundland dog with eyes that glow in the dark.

Accounts of spectral black dogs are also numerous in England and phantasms, sometimes described as Newfoundland dogs, have been reported at various times in Stogursey, a ruined monastery in Somerset on the sea road from St. Audries to Perry Farm.

In the *Book of Days*, published in 1879, a correspondent describes how a chimney sweep had drowned an old woman he suspected of witchcraft. The sweep was gibbeted near the scene of his crime and afterward, so it was said, the spot was haunted by a large, black, ghostly dog, described as being "not unlike a Newfoundland dog." The antagonistic haunt was described as emaciated and shaggy, with eyes of fire and fearsome teeth. He would make his appearance, then after a short time, vanish like a shadow.

Not all legends of Newfoundland dogs are frightening, of course. In 1813, during the seemingly endless series of squabbles between England and France, a privateer under the command of Captain Jacques de Bon captured an English fishing vessel and its crew on the Grand Banks. Why he did so is a puzzle, as de Bon treated his prisoners with every kindness and had his men repair the damage they had caused to the English ship.

When the repairs were finished, he set the English crew free and, as a parting gift, gave them a dog he had stolen from Newfoundland. Around the dog's neck the French captain tied a ship's biscuit, a symbolic gesture meaning that he would not keep a brother's dog in bondage nor see him want for bread. The Poole fishing merchant who owned the ship had the biscuit varnished to preserve it and then framed it. Today that famous bit of hard bread is still on display at the Lodge of Amity at Poole, in Dorset, England.

Another legendary Newfoundland, Boatswain, taken to England as a puppy by a Royal Navy captain in 1800, changed the course of world history a few times. His story is fairly well known, but is described in especial detail by Karin Broennecke. At the age of two, Boatswain was presented to Prince George Augustus Frederick, the future Prince Regent, who later became George IV. A letter described him as the most beautiful dog of his breed, with a spotted coat of steel grey and brown, a majestic head, eyes full of fire and yet gentleness, and a beautifully shaped, broad tail that was permanently in motion.

Without Boatswain, British prime minister William Pitt's alliance of the European nations against France would not have been formed and the Battle of Waterloo would not have taken place. One evening in 1804 there was a reception for diplomats accredited to the Court of St. James at Carlton House in London. Rumours to the effect that England was on the verge of breaking its alliance with France had begun; nevertheless, the French envoy and the ambassador who had come from Paris especially for this occasion were chatting away nonchalantly.

Prussia was to be the final member of the alliance Pitt was endeavouring to create, and the presence of the French representatives assured the neutrality and goodwill of the Prussian envoy. While Prince George tried in vain to convince the Prussian of the advantages of an alignment with England, Boatswain entered the room, his tail waving cheerfully. The Prince noticed that he was carrying something and called him over, whereupon the dog presented him with a letter.

The missive had been dropped on the floor of the nearby salon and, as the Prince handed the letter to the Prussian delegate, he saw the French envoy searching his pockets; the letter had been directed to him. The Prussian read:

> Monsieur, I am writing to my envoy at the same time, the matter is of utmost importance. Any rapprochement between the Court of St. James and the Prussian envoy must—at all costs—be prevented. The latter is a man of a silly and complacent nature. You will have no difficulty in dealing with him.
> Bonaparte, First Consul.

A month or so afterward, the first alliance against France and its tyrannical Corsican leader had been ratified.

Some time later the prince gave Boatswain to his close friend George "Beau" Brummel, the well-known dandy. Before long Brummel, always in debt because of his gambling, sold the dog to the Duke of Richmond for £7500. Eventually Boatswain, a favourite of all, went to live with the famous explorer and scholar Admiral

Sir John Ross. Ross was soon given permission to visit France and he took the dog with him. While there, he was granted an audience with Napoleon at St. Cloud. The dog accompanied him and the Emperor made much of him.

Upon Napoleon's first abdication in 1814, the island of Elba was ceded to him and he was exiled there. From that moment his supporters and friends from better days made plans to take him back to France, where veteran soldiers of his many campaigns were ready to put him back on the throne.

Meanwhile, Boatswain, through some sort of legacy, had become the dog of another Royal Navy captain, who now commanded a ship anchored off Elba. As he and his dog were walking on the island the captain was surprised to meet the ex-emperor and was rather taken aback when his dog rushed up to Napoleon and greeted him gleefully. Napoleon remembered the Newfoundland and treated him like a long-lost friend, even remembering his name.

On the night of March 1, 1815, during the commotion of a thunderstorm, a boat came to Elba's rocky shore to take Napoleon to the ship that was to land him in France. An English spy was also taken prisoner and brought on board by some French officers. As Napoleon stepped onto the deck of the boat, he slipped and fell into the deep water. In the darkness, excitement, and confusion, his disappearance went unnoticed for a long moment.

Napoleon, a poor swimmer at the best of times and overweight after months of inactivity during his exile, flailed about helplessly. He was doomed unless someone came to his aid, and his friends couldn't even see him.

He sank twice. Then, from out of the darkness sprang a huge shadow, Boatswain. The dog gripped the sinking Corsican's collar and held his head above water while he dragged him to the boat, where he was pulled to safety.

It transpired that the English prisoner was Boatswain's latest master, the captain of the offshore vessel, who had been arrested as a spy as he attempted to return from a visit ashore. As a token of his gratitude Napoleon took Boatswain and the captain in his retinue until they reached Paris, from whence they were escorted to Boulogne. There they were put on board an English frigate and taken home.

Boatswain returned to his former residence at Windsor Castle with the Prince Regent and heir to the throne. The elderly dog died some months later and a marble memorial was erected in his honour on the castle grounds. Much inconvenience would have been avoided had this heroic and well-intentioned dog remained in the boat on that fateful spring day.

Perhaps the most familiar Newfoundland dog story is that of Lord Byron and his dog, yet another Boatswain. Considered one of the greatest poets of the English Romantic Era, Byron is also known for his devotion to his Newfoundland, and vice versa. Some have speculated that the dog was given to him by his grandfather, Vice Admiral John Byron, Governor of Newfoundland from 1769 to 1772. Since the admiral died in 1786, seventeen years before Boatswain was born, according to the inscription on the latter's monument, how Byron came by the dog is unknown.

Lord Byron's fabled Boatswain, c.1806.

Boatswain succumbed to hydrophobia, better known today as rabies. On November 18, 1808, in what was thought to be a display of atheistic rebelliousness, Byron had him placed in a vault or, as some sources say, buried, at Newstead Abbey, Nottinghamshire. The inscription on the tomb, once attributed to Byron himself, is now thought to have been written by his close friend John Cam Hobhouse. It reads:

> Near this spot
> are deposited the remains of one
> who possessed Beauty without Vanity,
> Strength without Insolence,
> Courage without Ferocity,
> and all the Virtues of Man without his Vices.
> This Praise, which would be unmeaning Flattery
> if inscribed over human ashes,
> is but just tribute to the Memory of
> BOATSWAIN, a DOG
> who was born in Newfoundland May 1803
> and died at Newstead Nov. 18th, 1808.

Apparently Joseph Murray, one of Byron's servants, was interred with the dog and Byron intended that he and his butler William Fletcher would join them.

Fletcher announced that he was leaving Byron's service because, "Your Lordship will be buried in the Westminster Abbey. That leaves Boatswain and myself to be buried under the monument. At Judgement Day what will they think of me On High when I rise from the same grave as a dog? No thank you. I am leaving."

An additional inscription on the memorial is dated November 30, 1808:

> When some proud Son of Man returns to Earth,
> Unknown to Glory, but upheld by Birth,
> The sculptor's art exhausts the pomp of woe,
> And storied urns record who rests below:
> When all is done, upon the Tomb is seen,
> Not what he was, but what he should have been
> …Ye! who perchance behold this simple urn,
> Pass on—it honours none you wish to mourn:
> To mark a friend's remains these stones arise;
> I never knew but one—and here he lies.

After Boatswain's death Byron acquired another Newfoundland, Lyon, but in 1816 scandal forced Byron to flee England. He took his dog with him to Greece and in a sudden and incomprehensible desire to do something noble—and certainly unsafe—he devoted himself and his money to the Greek cause; he even sold his yacht. In 1823 he joined Greek insurrectionists against the Turks, who had occupied Greece for more than a hundred years.

Already sickly from a life of profligacy and frantic dieting to maintain his renowned good looks, Byron succumbed to a fever and died at the age of thirty-six in 1824, with Lyon at his bedside. Afterward the dog was taken to England, where he was cared for by a Mrs. Leigh for the rest of his life.

Other writers have been drawn to the Newfoundland dog. In 1820 Sir Walter Scott, being familiar with the Newfoundland's exploits, wrote in *The Sportsman's Repository*: "no other of the canine race [is] able to endure the water so long, or swim with so great facility." He also called him "the most useful of the whole canine race as far as hitherto known upon the face of the earth."

Edgar Allan Poe's *The Narrative of Arthur Gordon Pym*, written as a serial in 1837 and later reprinted in England, was his longest story, and to Poe's disappointment it failed to become popular. The story tells of a boy who stows away on a whaling ship, survives mutiny, savagery, cannibalism, and wild pursuit, and is always accompanied and aided by his loyal and sturdy Newfoundland dog, Tiger.

Pym explains that for seven years the dog has been his inseparable companion and in a multitude of instances "had given evidence of all the noble qualities for which we value the animal." Pym rescued Tiger when a puppy, from "the clutches of a malignant little villain in Nantucket who was leading him, with a rope around his neck, to the water; and the grown dog repaid the obligation, about three years afterward, by saving me from the bludgeon of a street robber."

Nana, the Darling children's babysitter in J. M. Barrie's *Peter Pan,* is a large Landseer. Unfortunately, when Sir James Barrie turned the book into a play, he traded the Landseer for a St. Bernard.

As mentioned, some stories about Newfoundlands may be outright lies, and this could very well be one of them. In his 1855 book, John Mulally talks to an old fisherman about the intelligence of the latter's gigantic Newfoundland, Sailor:

I never, said he, "seed such an animal. He beats any dog ever I com'd across all hollow, and as for sense, why I tell you he's got more than many Christians I have heerd of. If I was to tell you some things about that fellow," he continued, looking down at the dog which stood beside him, and patting him affectionately on the head, "you wouldn't believe me. Would they Sailor?" he said, addressing the animal, which looked up in his face with an expression which seemed to say as well as a dog could say, "I'm of your opinion exactly."

"Well, Gentlemen," proceeded the worthy fisherman, "you needn't believe me, but it's the truth I'm tellin'—that dog'll wake me up any hour of the morning that I tell him, and if I don't get up he'll pull me out of bed."

"Pull you out of bed!" said one of our party, with a smile of incredulity.

"Yes, sir, he'll pull me out of bed, and he's often done it afore now. But that's not all, gentlemen, that dog has gone a-fishin' just as nat'ral as any human bein'."

"Gone a-fishing," we all exclaimed with one voice.

"Yes, gentlemen, gone a-fishin'; and as I said afore, you needn't believe it if you don't like."

For the privilege which he gave us of doubting his word, we were of course duly thankful, and having expressed our utmost confidence in himself and respect for the wonderful accomplishments of "Sailor" we requested with proper feeling of reverence for both, to be enlightened upon the particular qualifications of the animal.

"Why, you see, I tell you how he does. He gets the line and after he baits the hooks he fastens one end of it on the shore and swims out with the other end some distance; then he drops it in the water. When he's done this he gets a piece of the line in his mouth and as soon as he feels the fish a-bitin' he gives it a sudden jerk and then swims ashore with him."

"Ah, yes, that's all very well," said one of his hearers, "but how does he get the hook out?"

"Well, you see he never lets the fish swallow the hook, and to prevent him from doin' so he catches him on the very first nibble. Oh, he's a cunnin' fellow, I tell you, gentlemen. Why if I was to tell you everythin' about him," he said, "you wouldn't believe me no more'n I was tellin' you a pack of lies."

We assured him we had every confidence in his veracity, adding that there was no reason why we should not, as we had some dogs in the United States which were taught the dumb alphabet. This was as far as a proper regard for truth would allow us to go, but the reputation of our country was at stake, and we were determined that its powers of "invention" should be fully sustained.

—from Mulally, *A Trip to Newfoundland*

Even more likely to fall into the realm of legend is a report made by the city marshal of Farmersville, some forty miles northeast of Dallas, Texas, in 1896. There had been an eruption of strange and inexplicable sightings of flying machines over the entire United States. The marshal described a "cigar-shaped airship" that flew over him at an altitude of about two hundred feet and scared the living daylights out of residents. It was not at all encouraging to have the marshal report that in it he saw two men and "something resembling a large Newfoundland dog."

Another colourful story was told around 1955 by Arthur Downey, a schoolteacher from Winterton, Newfoundland. According to Downey, a hunter had trained his Newfoundland dog to retrieve and claimed that when he sent his dog into the brush to fetch a partridge, the dog usually brought one back—not necessarily shot by his owner and not necessarily dead.

To prove his point he ordered the dog to fetch, and it ran off into the woods. Time dragged on but the hunter asserted his dog would be successful. It took an hour or more and when his dog returned he was carrying a box of Browning Harvey's biscuits. (For non-Newfoundlanders: the trademark on these boxes was a partridge, better known as a willow grouse.)

Last on our list of legends is the story of the rescue of the crew and passengers from the SS *Ethie*. There are many different versions of the events, and over the time the story has become so convoluted it is difficult to discern exactly what happened.

On December 11, 1919, the steamer was caught in a fierce storm and was in danger of going to pieces. Captain Edward English, in a calculated but desperate attempt to save the ship and its passengers, ran *Ethie* aground near Martins Point, twelve miles north of Bonne Bay on Newfoundland's west coast.

The popular version of the story is that a lifeline was shot to shore but failed to reach it, falling into the boiling surf, and efforts by the crew to get the passengers safely ashore proved futile. In a last-ditch attempt they sent the captain's Newfoundland dog, Tang, over the side with a line in his mouth, to swim to shore where rescuers were waiting to rig a lift or breeches buoy*.

Tang accomplished his task through a seething, storm-tossed sea, and ninety-three people were saved—thirty crewmen and sixty-three passengers, including an eighteen-month-old baby brought ashore in a mailbag. It is believed the number of people saved because of one Newfoundland's courage was a record for any dog of any breed. The most widespread version of the story has Tang being given a Meritorious Service medal from Lloyd's of London, which he is said to have worn on his collar until he died in St. John's of old age. (E. J. Pratt, in his poem based on the event, for some odd reason, called the dog Carlo.)

Other accounts of the *Ethie*'s trouble contend that someone on shore, who may have been a fisherman, commanded his dog, which may have been a Newfoundland, to swim out to the ship. The dog was supposedly thrown a line by the crew and he returned with it to shore. Also, McBurney and Byers state in *True Newfoundlanders* that "one of the men, Reuben Decker, sent out his Newfoundland dog, which brought the buoy safely ashore."

Yet another version claims that as the vessel was going to pieces on the shore, Reuben Decker and his work dog Wisher were emerging from a droke* with a load of firewood. Decker ran for help, followed by Wisher, who had broken free from his—or, her, according to writer Cassie Brown—harness. Meanwhile, the crew of the *Ethie* had attached a line to a buoy, which they succeeded in getting close enough to shore for livyers* to hook it with a stick. A heavier line was fastened to it and pulled back to the ship. On the beach Decker helped hold the life-saving rope that had been brought in while Wisher barked and ran around the legs of the rescuers, making a nuisance of himself. All the passengers made it safely to shore.

The late Cassie Brown, widely recognized as an authority on the *Ethie* wreck, interviewed both First Mate John Gullage and Reuben Decker, and they described Wisher as a small yellowish "collie type," and as a "little yellow cross-breed collie." (Quoted in Cranford, *Seadogs & Skippers.*)

Paul O'Neill writes in his *Breakers: Stories from Newfoundland and Labrador* first that Wisher was a mastiff, and a little further on, a mongrel. More recently, Garry Cranford said that a photograph purported to be of Wisher showed her to look remarkably like a cross between a collie and a Newfoundland. This is almost an exact description of the Newfoundland dogs of an earlier era, so perhaps the hero of the rescue was in fact a Newfoundland.

Brown said that during her interview with Gullage he explained how the legend of a Newfoundland dog rescuer was born. Apparently, when the survivors of the wreck were on a train to Deer Lake, the ship's chief engineer, Paddy Burton, in "a fit of devilment" spun a fantastic yarn of being rescued by a sturdy Newfoundland carrying a lifeline.

The dog was actually awarded a collar bearing a silver plate with the word "Hero" engraved on it, and fastened to it were two medals. The first was engraved "Presented to Hero by Starry Cross of Philadelphia, Pa, in token of appreciation for his rescue of 92 souls from the *Ethie* on December 10th 1919," with the number 92 on the obverse. The second was inscribed, "Presented to HERO by the sick soldiers of Camp Hill Hospital, Halifax, NS, May 7th, 1923." Whatever the truth, the following appeared in a New Brunswick newspaper on July 26, 1922:

A fine collar with a cross attached arrived today for "Hero," the Newfoundland dog owned by William Cramm of this city in recognition of saving 93 lives in the wreck of the steamship *Ethie* on 10 December 1919, on the coast of Newfoundland. The dog swam through waves taking a line ashore from the ship, and by means of this, a heavier line was put aboard and all saved. The collar and cross are from the Starry Cross Society of Philadelphia. Mayor McLennan has exempted "Hero" from paying the local dog tax.

—quoted in Brown, *Newfoundland Journeys*

The name "Cramm" is probably a misinterpretation of the hand-written "Orum," as Decker sold both Wisher and the collar—at $30 each—to the opportunist William Orum of Saint John, New Brunswick. Since Orum wanted to take the dog on an exhibition tour, perhaps he bought an impressive Newfoundland dog to go with the collar, as it would have made a much more compelling show. Anyway, collar, dog, and Orum disappeared.

We next hear of the collar in 1923, when it showed up complete with medals and large dog at Wrangell, Alaska, in the possession of one Dennis "Dinty" Kane, who had come from New Brunswick. Sue Bradley, daughter of U.S. Marshall C. W. "Shorty" Bradley and a one-time resident of Wrangell, remembered the big brown-black dog that she called King. He often slept next to her stove on cold nights as Kane, who worked around the Cassiar gold fields in northwest British Columbia and the Yukon, lived in a shack that the dog apparently deemed too cold and primitive for his taste.

The young Bradley was delighted to have a large friendly dog as a playmate, and she is one of the few who have any memory of Kane, who died at Wrangell in 1931 under shady circumstances. He was buried in the local cemetery and the *Wrangell Sentinel* printed his obituary on July 10.

Sue Bradley doesn't remember the demise of the dog but she recalled seeing the collar and its medals when she was a teenager. Shorty Bradley stashed the collar away in a steamer trunk when he moved his family to Talkeetna. After Shorty's death in 1966, the trunk was left with his wife, Florence, who moved back to Wrangell.

Somehow, the trunk ended up in the possession of a Jim Lovett and he kept it in the attic of an old house there. Charlotte Moody, while cleaning out the house in 1982, found the trunk and took its contents to the dump, except for the collar and medals. She gave these to Dottie Olson, a collector of odds and ends, who hung them above the bar at Dottie's Roadhouse Lodge.

The story resurfaced in the press on October 21, 2000. A headline appeared in the Saint John's *Telegram* that read: "Heroic dog's collar on loan to museum." The story reads:

A Newfoundland at about the time of the SS *Ethie* disaster, as depicted in Edward Drinker Cope's *Natural History*, c.1875.

The collar that belonged to the Newfoundland dog which played a major role in a high seas rescue off the west coast in 1919 has been loaned to the Newfoundland Museum.

The collar came all the way from Alaska, where the dog last lived with its master.

The dog was a hero in the rescue of 92 passengers and crew on the S.S. *Ethie*, which ran aground during a December 1919 storm off Cow head. The dog swam out to the strickened vessel to catch a line and bring it back to shore to start the rescue.

In 2002, the account of the historic "Hero" collar reappeared in the *Newfoundland Herald*. The story goes that the dog moved to New Brunswick then, with a new owner, to Alaska, where the two remained for the rest of their lives.

Olson found the story of the *Ethie* through a website set up by a Bruce and Anna Ricketts of Ottawa. She contacted them and they eventually agreed to lend the collar to the Newfoundland Museum. When then-Minister of Tourism, Culture and Recreation Charles "Chuck" J. Furey accepted the collar from the Rickettses on behalf of Newfoundland and Labrador, he commented, "It's wonderful when such a unique object is repatriated to Newfoundland so that it can be exhibited at the Newfoundland Museum."

The presentation, which took place in the minister's office, was attended by Penny Houlden, curator of the Newfoundland Museum, and Hilda Menchions of St. John's. In 1919, she was Hilda Batten of Bareneed, the baby saved from the *Ethie* wreck by being slipped into the mailbag and sent ashore.

Today, some few rusting bits of the *Ethie*'s corpse can still be seen on the foreshore at Martins Point. There have been many accounts of and not a few books written about this subject. Bruce Ricketts is probably the authority on the shipwreck today, but the argument may never be settled to the satisfaction of all. Myth or not, the convoluted story of the *Ethie* is one of the numerous examples of how Newfoundland dogs have affected many lives.

For the doggie who comes from Newfoundland.

From Father Tuck's Nursery Series, *Cock-a-Doodle Do!*

Chapter 5

Devoted Friend

Woodrow Wilson once said, "If a dog will not come to you after he has looked you in the face, you should go home and examine your conscience." However, the devotion of the Newfoundland to its owner is unconditional and legendary, and has been demonstrated many times.

From 1770 to 1786, George Cartwright lived in Labrador and kept a detailed diary of his experiences and travels, entitled *A Journal of Transactions and Events during a Residence of nearly Sixteen Years on the Coast of Labrador*. His first post was established at Cape Charles, where he became friends with the Inuit. From here he made many fishing, trapping, and exploratory treks.

[Tuesday, January 29, 1771] Guy pursued the track to the mouth of Niger Sound, and upon the North End of Round Island he found the unfortunate Mr. Jones frozen to death, with his faithful Newfoundland bitch at his side! He gave the poor creature what bread he had about him but could not prevail on her to leave her master.

[Thursday, January 31, 1771] The Chateau men went off for Seal Island early this morning; from which place my man returned today, accompanied by those whom I sent from Chateau; also another party from the same place, joined them upon the road. These people brought me what things they found in Mr. Jones' pockets, and informed me that they had covered the corpse with snow and boughs of trees; but they could not prevail on the Newfoundland bitch to leave her deceased master.

The dog's pathetic faithfulness is heartbreaking and Cartwright's attitude is astonishing. The implied esteem, coming from a man devoted to the hunt and who was usually ready to kill anything that crossed his path, attests to his being favourably impressed. There's no further word of her fate.

—from Townsend,
Captain Cartwright and his Labrador Journal

Eliza Gilbert, better known to the world as the tempestuous actress and dancer Lola Montez, became a Newfoundland devotee by chance, and was lucky to have the dog. She was walking in London's Hyde Park in May 1849 when she saw a young man drive by in a carriage with a huge Newfoundland dog sitting beside him. She discovered the man was Cornet* George T. Heald of the 2nd Regiment of the Life Guards. Animal-lover Montez was so impressed she attempted to buy the dog, but instead she married Heald two months later. From that point on she was accompanied by the dog, even at the Hotel de Londres, in Boulogne, where he shared her suite.

Her marriage to Heald collapsed and Montez went on to other turbulent affairs and adventures, but she was seldom ever without her Newfoundland. Whether or not it was the same dog, it is impossible to say.

According to the *Panama Herald* of May 6, 1853, the beauteous and eccentric Montez visited Panama, and while at Gorgona, demanded the hotel manager set up a cot for her dog in her room.

The man argued that all his cots were in use and that her dog could sleep on the floor.

The irascible Montez removed her cigar from her mouth, stamped her foot, and told the manager that she cared not a whit where the other guests slept, but he'd better get a cot at once. The hotelier did as he was told, but next morning added a five dollar charge to Montez's bill, insisting she pay it. She refused, emphasizing her point by whipping out a pistol and threatening to settle not only the bill but his hash.

The *San Francisco Bulletin* reported that she hadn't changed much when, in November 1855, she attempted to stab the mate of the SS *Fanny Major* for kicking her dog.

In the summer of 1859, Montez was reported wandering about London, muttering to herself and reading the Bible to anyone who would listen. Her final religious mania had begun. One day she was sitting in Regent's Park, a tired figure in black, reading the New Testament, with a big Newfoundland dog beside her. When a reporter asked her if she was Lola Montez, she answered, "Who I am is no matter." It certainly didn't matter to the dog, who remained loyal to her through good times and bad.

Booth Chern recounts yet another story of profound dedication in *The New Complete Newfoundland*. A Newfoundland dog's master hanged himself at Salem, Massachusetts. The police were permitted by the big dog to cut the man down, but when they tried to take the body away, the Newfoundland, bent on protecting his owner, ferociously attacked them. The police rapidly retreated and the mourning dog licked his master's face. Each time the police tried to get near, the dog growled and drove them off. Sadly, in their attempt to remove the man's body the police killed the faithful guardian, using fourteen bullets to put an end to his efforts.

Perhaps one of the oddest accounts of the behaviour of a Newfoundland was printed in the *New York World* in the late 1800s. Unaccountably, Nero had been whipped by a bad-tempered owner for tearing a little girl's dress when they were playing. The dog's sensitivities had been profoundly offended and he refused to eat. A short time later, he was killed by the West Shore Railroad's 4:15 p.m. train. The newspaper article reads like a melodrama from the silent film era, and we're not qualified to say it wasn't so:

> Not an engineer on the West Shore Railroad, familiar with the daily sight of a magnificent Newfoundland pacing beside a train or giving it a lordly greeting as it passed by, would dispute the popular contention.
>
> "Why that dog knew as much about a train as the best man alive," said the trainman. "Suicide?" said the engineer of the 4:15, "Why, it was as plain a case—as you ever heard of. I felt just as bad as if I had struck a man, it took all the nerve out of me."
>
> "There he was across the track, his head resting on the rail." Never had he done such a thing before.
>
> "His tail never quivered as the engine approached. He was steeled for the death stroke. His eyes were sad and he licked his lips. As I saw him going under the pilot I shut my eyes and groaned. I could feel the pilot wheel cutting off that noble head."
>
> —quoted in Booth Chern,
> *The New Complete Newfoundland*

What anyone would hope to gain by spinning such a yarn is beyond comprehension; on the other hand it's difficult to believe it could be true.

Newfoundlands are noted for their intellect, but sometimes their sense of discrimination and fair play seems to be lacking. The following was included in an 1871 treatise by Ernest Menault's:

> An individual, whom, from regard to his honour, we forbear to name, had an old Newfoundland dog, which, for economy's sake, he wished to get rid of, to save the dog tax. This man, with a view of executing his cruel design, led his old servant to the banks of the Seine, tied his paws together with string, and rolled him off the barge into the current. The dog, in struggling, contrived to break his bonds, and managed, with great difficulty to climb the steep bank of the river, where he arrived almost breathless. Here his unworthy master awaited him with a stick. He repulsed the animal, and struck him violently; but, in the effort, lost his balance and fell into the river. He would have drowned most assuredly, had not his dog been more humane than himself. But the animal, faithful to the natural mission of his race, and forgetting in a moment the treatment he had just received, jumped into the water from which he had only just escaped, to rescue his would-be executioner from death. He did not accomplish this task without much difficulty; and both returned home—the one meekly rejoicing at having accomplished a good deed and obtained favour, the other disarmed and, let us hope, repentant.
>
> —from Menault, *The Intelligence of Animals*

Dr. R. M. Nelson, a native of Truro, Nova Scotia, moved to Newfoundland in the late 1860s. In those days most wintertime travel was on foot or by dogsled across the rugged land. Rigorous winters added to the hazards of touring about the countryside, and most emergencies could be counted upon to happen during extreme conditions.

During the drive from Blackhead to Carbonear, twelve miles to the southeast, on January 16, 1870, Nelson had his legs so badly frozen that they later had to be amputated. His life was saved only by the presence of his big Newfoundland dog, which remained with him and kept him warm through his ordeal. The next year Nelson began medical practice at Carbonear, but he later moved to Western Bay, Bay de Verde, where he ministered to the sick for twenty years. He died there on January 5, 1906. One can only imagine how many of his patients would have suffered if his Newfoundland hadn't saved his life.

The Newfoundland as portrayed by J. G Millais around 1900, around the time of Neptune.

A story in the *New York Times* in the early 1900s (retold by Booth Chern in *The New Complete Newfoundland*) tells of Neptune, who belonged to Captain Stephen Lemist and who was highly regarded by all the crew. Neptune had complete freedom aboard Lemist's ship and sometimes walked along a rail or ventured to some other position that many would consider unsafe; his agility and sense of balance usually saw him safely through. His vessel, bound for New Orleans and fifty miles below that port in the vicinity of Port Sulphur, was being towed up the Mississippi River when the ship lurched. Neptune, walking along a rail at the time, had tempted fate once too often. He lost his balance and went over the side.

Lemist couldn't stop without possibly disastrous complications with the tow, so he had to leave his dog to make out as best he could. The dog swam after his ship for some time, then made for the river bank. His shipmates were heartsick and it was said that Lemist wept openly.

Three days later, Lemist's ship was berthed alongside other ships while loading tobacco and cotton at a Crescent City wharf. Suddenly, Neptune leapt onto the deck. He had travelled the fifty miles upstream, crossed the water at some point close to New Orleans, found his way to the docks, then scrambled across two tiers of vessels to get to his ship. How did he find it? Once again, the almost magical connection between man and dog had asserted itself.

Another case of a Newfoundland finding its way home had a tragic ending. Late in 1963, Sylvia and Winthrop Wadleigh's 180-pound Moxie was outside near their home in Manchester, New Hampshire. Having heard a truck stop nearby and Moxie's barking, Sylvia hurried outside, but their dog was gone and there was the lingering scent of ether. It didn't take great deductive powers to figure out what had happened. A search for the dog and a subsequent investigation disclosed that an old truck filled with dogs had stopped at the local animal shelter asking about large dogs. A five-month hunt through the United States and Canada turned up nothing, though a reward was offered. They received many telephone calls, but all came to naught.

Then, one morning, Sylvia went outside, and there was Moxie at the back door. He appeared to have been starved, his pads were badly worn from miles of travel, and his coat was matted and filled with twigs and burs. Perhaps only the thieves know how far he had to travel to reach home and, sadly, he had come home to die and passed away soon after.

If anyone doubts the courage of Newfoundland dogs and the affection they hold for all creatures, particularly their own masters, the many stories of their actions should convince them.

Chapter 6

A Working Dog's Life

Behind the soft, gentle, facade of the Newfoundland is an elemental raw power. Excellent draught animals, they respond to vocal directions exceptionally well, and up until the 1920s it was quite usual to see a single dog or a team deliver a load, then turn about and return by themselves. They once pulled loads of fish from stages* and beaches to the stores, and were often seen drawing carts bearing all sorts of articles on Newfoundland roads. They hauled firewood and timber from the forest, and around town delivered merchandise and supplies, often making their excursions unaccompanied.

Aaron Thomas of HMS *Boston*, rated only as an able seaman, though he was probably the captain's steward or clerk, kept a diary of his 1794–1795 voyage from England to Newfoundland and back. There is much embroidery in his narrative, and sometimes there's uncertainty where it begins and ends. Nevertheless, it may give a good idea of the amount of work a Newfoundland was really expected to do.

Sunday, May 25 [1794]: I was ashore at St. John's...From the human specie I shall proceed to treat to a different kind, I mean Dogs—in this Country a most useful animal indeed.

The celebrity of Newfoundland Dogs in England is so notorious that the value of them there needs no comment, but their usefulness in Britain cannot be put in competition with the great utility they are to the people of this cold Country… The people then cut their wood for firing, for Fish Flakes and for Building etc., etc. This wood is sometimes cut seven or ten miles in the woods and is drawn by Dogs…This labour of Dogs is daily thro the winter and a hard service it is…

…They kept in herds or companys the same as Bears and Wolves do now. In winter they lived by hunting and killing Foxes, Beavers, etc., and when these failed them they had recourse to the watery element, which never refused them relief, for if the neighbouring Seas were frozen over they would perambulate on the Ice on which they would find Sea Lions, Seals and other animals that became an easy prey when attack'd by a formidable host of these Dogs.

In Summertime they follow'd the same business of Hunting and when the woods deny'd them food the Sea Shore became their rendezvous. Here they catched Fish to suffer their wants and when nature was satisfy'd they betook themselves again to their haunts in the woods, where they had nothing to fear from rivals, going generally in such numerous herds that flocks of Wolves would shun them. I am told that in winter these Dogs were the greatest enemys to themselves, for when on the Barrens their food began to get short they would, as their appetites increas'd, set up a dismal howl, and this noise of theirs would continue untill they arriv'd at the Sea Shore. Before they reached the Beach they might a travelled several miles, but before they began their march they collect'd in great numbers, four of five hundred in a drove. Everyone of these would give his yell and the horrible Harmony produc'd by this tumultuous assemblage must, no doubt, strike terror into every Animal within the limits of the frightfull sound. Thus Beasts, who otherwise might have become their prey had they travelled orderly and quietly like peacefull citizens, made all haste in their power to escape from so piercing a clangour.

These Dogs, in Summer, lead the perfect life of an Idler. They do no kind of work whatever. These poor Creatures, lean and meager, all day lye like lifeless carcasses in the Sun; when night comes they prowl about under the Fish Flakes in great numbers, quarrelling and fighting with all the stragglers of their own species that they meet, and yet they seem now so much degenerated from their ancient character that nothing now remains of their former good qualities, except that of Diving and their strength and agility for drawing wood, for they are at this period as great a brood of cowards as any of that kind of specie. I doubt not but that one single English Bull Dog would put to flight a Posse of twenty or thirty of them.

October, 1794: A banker[*] is not a little proud of his Dog at Sea. This Creature exhibited his dexterity and usefullness to a surprizing degree. In addition to what I have stated before in the History of Newfoundland Dogs I shall mention the following trait as a good quality in their composition. The Fishermen, when they hooked a Fish, in drawing the line up the Fish sometimes disentangled themselves. The Fish may sometimes float on the Water. The Dog, observing this, dasheth into the Sea and brings the Fish alongside. They then throw a Rope out and the Dog, with the Fish in his mouth, puts Head into the Noose of the Rope and Fish and Dog are hauled into the Vessel together. At Sea those Dogs often persue and kill Water Fowl. I have heard of a Dog who was absent from a Ship on the Grand Bank for Two days, on the Third he return'd with a Hegdown [a sea bird] in his mouth. These Dogs have also been seen to dive after Porpoises but without success.

—from Murray,
The Newfoundland Journal of Aaron Thomas (1794)

In 1824 more than two thousand Newfoundlands were employed in St. John's alone and a working dog's monetary worth was estimated to be £4500 to £5000! It is therefore not surprising that decrees to get rid of them were often ignored.

Teams of six or seven Newfoundlands carried the mail and, unlike most other dog teams, where the driver ran along behind the sled, such a team of the big dogs could cover a great distance, sometimes as much as seventy miles (112 kilometres) in a day, with assorted goods *and* with the driver riding. Sometimes there was a passenger or two as well! The Newfoundlands never failed to deliver the mail, and for this service they were said to have been honoured by appearing on Newfoundland postage stamps. However, the teams that delivered most of the mail were usually of a mixed breed, or of the mongrel variety, as the terrain was often too rough for the much heavier

A St. John's street scene from around 1900 shows the common practice of hitching Newfoundlands to sleds.

Newfoundlands; these travelled shorter distances but with considerably larger loads.

The Lewis and Clark Expedition of 1804–1806, led by Captain Meriwether Lewis and Second Lieutenant William Clark, travelled from St. Louis, Missouri, to the Pacific and back. Lewis and Clark's expedition was one of the most important explorations of what is now the continental United States. Accompanying them was the now-famous Newfoundland known as "Scannon."

When Donald Jackson recently studied the toponymy of the area he noticed that among those features named by Lewis and Clark in Montana was a "Seaman's Creek." Captain Lewis had named this northern tributary of the Blackfoot River in 1806, and Jackson's research established that the group's system of naming was unsophisticated and was usually inspired by members of the party or its sponsors. Jackson couldn't reconcile the name "Seaman" with other reports and at first thought it was a spelling error and should have been "Scannon."

After examining the expedition's journals he found the creek was correctly named, and the dog's name was in fact Seaman. The handwritten error is apparent when pointed out: the *e* appeared as a *c*, and the *m* was taken to be two *n*'s, then it was assumed the final *a* was an *o*; thus we had "Scannon."

Setting out in March the expedition travelled by keel-boat, canoe, and on foot, and took with them the dog we now know to be Seaman, Lewis' Newfoundland. A working member of the party, the dog accompanied them to the Pacific and Fort Clatsop at the mouth of the Columbia River and back.

Soon after their departure a Shawnee attempted to trade Lewis three beaver skins for the dog, but he was turned down. Lewis wrote in his journal, "I prized him much for his docility and qualifications generally for my journey and, of course, there was no bargain."

Seaman carried equipment and supplies on his back or hauled them, retrieved game shot by the party (in one instance he killed and brought back an antelope), and guarded the camps against animals. An entry in Lewis' journal read: "The white bears [silver-tip grizzly bears] have now become exceedingly troublesome; they constantly infest our camp during the night, though they have not attacked us, as our dog who patrols all night gives us notice of the approach." Lewis also wrote in his journal that though equipment for his expedition was important, a more vital element was the men accompanying him. He stated that apart from Clark, Seaman was the only other member of his party that he had confidence in.

The extreme weather of the winter of 1804–1805 brought difficulties, and the Chinook First Nations took advantage of the situation to plague the expedition day in and day out. The last straw for Lewis was when they captured Seaman. Lewis sent three men to recover his dog and ordered them to fire on the thieves if they showed any reluctance to return him; the dognappers fled, leaving the dog behind. Seaman is a member of the group as depicted by the Lewis and Clark monument at Kansas City, Missouri, and his name is also recorded (unfortunately, as Scannon) at Fort Clatsop on a bronze plaque, as one of the party to make the entire journey. (This story is told in more detail in Lewis and Clark, *The Lewis and Clark Journals: An American Epic of Discovery*.)

In his book *Arctic Explorations*, Dr. Elisha Kent Kane records that when he set out to look for Franklin's lost expedition on May 30,

1853, he took ten Newfoundlands and the workaday huskies. Unlike the huskies, the Newfoundlands were easily directed by commands and, gentle and easily handled, they were harnessed abreast. Six of them made a powerful team and travelled with ease pulling a loaded sled. He observes that he had little difficulty with cracks in the ice, as the Newfoundlands leapt them, the sled being carried across by sheer inertia.

When gold was discovered at Bonanza Creek on the Klondike River, Yukon Territory, in 1896, the need for dogs in the area was overwhelming. The demand by would-be miners scraped the northwest nearly bare of anything remotely canine. When the Canadian government was getting dog teams together for the mail run to Dawson City, a hundred huskies were expected, but only forty could be ac-

The Newfoundland dog was an important part of the industry in the Yukon during the Klondike Gold Rush of 1898.

quired. Of those, only half were huskies, and the rest a mixed lot of "outside dogs"—setters, retrievers, collies, St. Bernards, and, of course, Newfoundlands. In other words, the motley crew consisted of any sturdy dog with a coat sufficient to allow them to survive the rigours of weather.

While huskies served many purposes, the Newfoundlands proved indispensable in drawing the heavy loads and were particularly valued. Old photos show them hauling freight and huge piles of logs in an area where roads were non-existent and the country nearly impossible for horses to traverse. One man, a water carrier, had a team of five black Newfoundlands that drew a cask fitted with a sort of axle by which it could be drawn over the ground like a roller. He made a substantial living delivering to homes and businesses.

When navigation opened in the spring of 1900, the Canadian Development Company had more than five hundred dogs of all descriptions on their hands. Since they would not be needed until winter set in again they were put on an island in Lake LaBarge, still called Dog Island today, and sent a dog-keeper there to care for them. After the company's horse-drawn service was properly organized, the dogs were all sold.

Mr. Deeds is a prime example of a working dog. He was owned by a Lieutenant Johnson of the Royal Air Force when he and his wife were stationed at Gander, Newfoundland, just prior to World War Two. One night in 1939 the Johnsons were entertaining, assisted by their maid, nineteen-year-old Muriel Goodyear. At some point, Johnson offered Muriel a glass of champagne (which she hated) and he announced, "Muriel is about to become a mother." Muriel was astonished to be presented with Deeds; unable to take the dog back to the

U.K. because of quarantine restrictions, he wanted to place him with a good owner. Muriel took the dog to her parents' home in Norris Arm and presented him to Calvin, her twelve-year-old brother.

Calvin's constant companion, Deeds pulled a sled each winter, hauling firewood and supplies. The sawmill at Amys Lake was eight miles from the Norris Arm post office and Deeds, with Calvin on the sled, would run the distance without stopping, pick up mail and other necessities, then run back to the mill. The return trip was mostly uphill, which didn't seem to bother Deeds at all.

Deeds knew a number of tricks, such as counting to ten and rolling over, but most of his skills were associated with work. Given a bag with a note in it he would to take it to the general store where a clerk filled the order, which Deeds would dutifully bring home. Calvin left home in 1948, and Deeds, having pulled a sled until the age of eighteen years, was retired to the logging camp when he became blind. There he continued his service by keeping bears away. The stout-hearted old dog died around 1960, at the age of at least twenty-one years and possibly close to twenty-three. He had never been overfed in his life, but probably had been overworked, and his longevity can likely be attributed to lots of exercise, good genes, and good luck.

During the International Geophysical Year of 1958, Japan sent an expedition to the Antarctic, as did many countries. When this group of highly intelligent scientists and technicians headed home in the fall, they for some reason left two of their sled dogs behind: Giro, a Greenland husky-type, and Taro, a large black Newfoundland.

Unbelievably, the two managed to find shelter and enough food to survive the horrendous Antarctic winter and were picked up the following year by another party. Giro did not live very long after being rescued, but Taro returned to Japan in 1961, where he became a national hero and lived to a ripe old age at the University Botanical Gardens in Hokkaido. He was much mourned after his death and both dogs were recently commemorated on Japanese postage stamps.

In the 1960s a farmer from Maine, Warren Thompson, had a dog named Bing who helped with chores on his isolated holdings. The big dog hauled hay and water for the livestock, brought in the cows, took firewood to the house, and helped out in many other ways.

Calamity struck in 1965, when Thompson's wife had an extended stay in the hospital and Thompson himself broke his leg. Now Bing proved his true worth. Hitched to his sled he took laundry to town and picked it up, visited the general store with a list of items to be brought home, got the mail, and fetched other things as needed.

Thompson, his leg in a cast, struggled through each day with his dog's help. One night, while a weary Thompson slept, an ember flew from the fireplace and set the floor alight. An alert Bing roused his owner, then helped him carry water from the brook to put the fire out before a great amount of damage was done.

Newfoundlands have not only served as mere draught animals, but they have been servants as well. In the early 1800s, a Newfoundland regularly took a basket and grocery list to a shop and picked up provisions for his owners. Known throughout the New England town, he was an object of civic pride. On his way to the store with an empty basket, he was never bothered. However, several smaller dogs invariably attacked him on his return trip, when his basket was full.

He wouldn't set his burden down where it would be endangered, so he had to bear the smaller dogs' assaults stoically, bringing his purchases home undamaged.

But one day he decided that enough was enough. He went through the motions of going to the shop with his basket and after the usual time had passed, he headed home. The other dogs received a terrific shock when he let his empty basket fall and gave them the thrashing of their lives. Corrective action having been taken, he picked up his basket and finished his errand. His commonsense approach to the problem was one of the things that led to his being commemorated by a pair of Parian (a pottery finish resembling marble) figurines that were quite popular at the time.

Uncommon errands for these dogs were a specialty, as Peter MacArthur reported in 1821. While eating breakfast with a friend on the north side of the bay at Falmouth, England, he was surprised by a large, wet Newfoundland that walked into the dining room and placed an oilcloth-wrapped package on the table. The friend explained that the dog swam across the bay every morning, picked up the packaged newspapers at the post office, and brought them home.

A Harbour Grace dog also had unique responsibilities. During the mid-1800s a magistrate of that town had a Newfoundland that carried his lantern for him when he ventured out at night. The dog did so as capably as any servant could have done and when the magistrate stopped, his dog stopped as well. When the magistrate resumed his walk, the dog again took up his position in front of him.

The magistrate's family found that when he had gone to town alone they could send the dog to get him. Given the lantern, the dog would set out for town, more than a mile away, and since he knew his master's friends he visited each of their homes. After setting his lantern down he growled at the door until someone opened it. If the magistrate wasn't there, he continued to the next house he was familiar with until he found him, and then lit his way home. One visit to a house with his master was reason enough for the dog to include it in his searches.

A wood cut of a Newfoundland dog, made in 1898 by an unknown artist.

One Newfoundland held down the job of doorman at a tavern on Argyle Street in Glasgow, Scotland. Around 1860 the establishment was well known, mostly because of the dog. He dutifully watched for patrons approaching the door, then trotted on ahead of them and rang the bell. That done, he returned to his post. His industry and behaviour brought many customers to the hostelry and he was well rewarded for his work.

According to Booth Chern, a Newfoundland, owned by an Autice Russell's Aunt Ida, carried out the duties of a household servant. He greeted each carriage that arrived at her home and if a lady alighted, the dog carefully picked up the hem of her long skirt and carried it as she walked up the steps and into the house, being very careful not to let it touch the ground.

Cluney MacPherson had a well-mannered dog named Jack who escorted the family's small children on their way to school and on their walks. He always kept himself between them and traffic and could also be trusted to pull a four-year-old in a two-wheeled cart or on a sled without upsetting the vehicle or frightening the child. When walking with his master he would carry a heavy package for long distances without resting and raised objections if MacPherson attempted to carry it. Even so, anyone else walking with them was quite welcome to pack the load.

Today, working dogs don't normally haul logs, fish, or mail, but some have jobs many people would envy. In 1964, NBC (National Broadcasting Company) made a documentary of the Lewis and Clark Expedition. Hard Tack (Ch. Little Bear's Hard Tack II) was brought in to play the role of Seaman. In April 3, 1965, the following piece by Lawrence Laurent appeared in the *Washington Post*:

> Yates [Ted Yates, the producer] hired a dog. It was a valuable champion but accustomed to the easy indolence of a Connecticut kennel. Yates insured the dog for $5000.
>
> "I like dogs," Yates continued, "but this one was more than four feet high and weighed over 200 pounds. It had an enormous requirement for water and a daily diet that required about five pounds of meat." Yates brought the dog to his Washington home, "to make friends."
>
> The thirsty animal promptly quenched his thirst by emptying all the water out of toilet bowls.
>
> "My kids," Yates added, "thought he was wonderful."
>
> The next morning, the dog was missing. Yates called the

police. A bored and sleepy desk sergeant said: "Okay, so you've lost a dog. Can you describe him?"

"Yes sir," answered Yates. "He's a Newfoundland...about four feet high...weighs over 200 pounds..."

The sergeant's boredom vanished, but all he could yell was "What?"

The dog was found quickly. Seems he had grown thirsty about dawn and had set out to find water. He had gone to DuPont Circle, where two sleepy gardeners were watering the grass. At the sight of the dog—about the size and shape of a small bear—the men had thrown down their hoses and fled.

The dog had drunk his fill. He had rolled around in the cool water, getting his heavy coat soaked. By this time, people had gathered at the DuPont Circle bus stop and the friendly animal loped over to the crowd. Then he shook himself dry and someone called the cops.

Hard Tack's favourite part of the whole movie-making business was shooting the rapids in a canoe. He sat bolt upright in the bow for every take and greatly enjoyed shooting the rapids and the upsets in the turbulent river.

One of Newfoundland's most popular tourist attractions is the ninety-foot-long banking schooner *Scademia*, operating out of St. John's. Converted to a seventy-five-passenger tour boat, it's skippered by Charlie Aronson, who created the first harbour tour of St. John's in 1978. The Adventure Tours' vessel has become a household name in Newfoundland as its "first mate," Bo'sun, is a Newfoundland dog that attracts as many tourists as the schooner does.

The *J & B*, a refurbished sixty-foot-long fishing schooner, also takes tourists on short voyages out of St. John's. Its skipper, Captain Austin Flynn, says his Newfoundland dog Sailor is an important part of the business. Besides attracting visitors, he barks at whales and doesn't mind having other dogs along to help him carry out his duties.

Gus, Bonavista's 190-odd-pound Newfoundland dog who passed away in 2003, was surely one of the most photographed dogs anywhere. He lived not far from the replica of Cabot's ship *Matthew* and was often shown sitting beside it or on it. His picture appeared in many publications and on postcards, shirts, posters, mugs and an assortment of other souvenirs.

Chapter 7

Sixth Sense

There must be some endowment of senses that dogs can have, beyond those known to science, that would explain some of the mysteries they create. To quote from G. K. Chesterton's prototypical dog in "The Song of Quoodle," they can sense "the smell of snare and warning." This theoretical concept suggests that more than man's simple "noselessness" is involved, and raises the question: Do dogs have extrasensory perception? Quoodle put it succinctly: "More than mind discloses, / And more than men believe."

In 1899, a Newfoundland dog was picked up swimming three hundred miles (483 kilometres) from the nearest point of land by a homeward-bound Gloucester fishing schooner. No other vessel was in sight and the dog, at first taken to be flotsam, then a body, was swimming vigorously toward them. His mysterious appearance was the subject of ceaseless conjecture for many years.

Taken back to Gloucester, he considered himself to be part of the crew and the schooner never sailed without him; he was a great favourite of all. The crew believed their dog was responsible for the good luck that followed them, because no matter how the schooner was fitted out or who skippered it, it was always among the highliners.*

As the time for sailing approached one season, the dog became restless. When the launching day arrived, his agitation was apparent to everyone. No amount of coaxing could get him to board the schooner, and he showed his disapproval by uncharacteristic loud barking. A crewman shrugged and said the trip would be a failure if the dog would not go, but his refusal had more significance than that. They sailed without him, rounded Eastern Point, and were never seen or heard of again.

The story of the Gloucester schooner and the mystery dog appeared in *Yankee Magazine* in June 1957. When O. M. Mosher of Mahone Bay, Nova Scotia, read it, it brought back memories and set his mind at ease over something he had pondered for years.

He was four years old in 1897 when his father, skipper of a fishing schooner, brought him a Newfoundland puppy, Prince. He grew to be a large and powerful dog and followed his young master most everywhere. When the boy fell through the ice, Prince was there to leap in and pull him out. The big dog played with the neighbourhood children, but his size and loud voice frightened some little girls, who complained to their mothers. Instead of telling them to stop being silly, their mothers complained to young Mosher's parents. To allay their fears, his father had one of the boy's uncles take the dog on his schooner, which was about to sail for the West Indies with a cargo of fish.

A month later the Mosher family received a letter to the effect that the dog had been lost overboard during a storm and the old, overloaded schooner was unable to turn about in the heavy seas to pick him up. Subsequently, Mosher's dog had been snatched from the water by the Gloucester schooner on an intersecting course, and he went on to become a legend in his new home.

In 1930, movie director Varrick Frissell began shooting the movie *The Viking* aboard the SS *Ungava*, and he was accompanied by his constant companion, Cabot. Frissell was unsatisfied with the result of the season's filming and in the following spring chartered Bowring's fifty-year-old, 510-ton SS *Viking* to shoot more footage.

They left St. John's on March 9 under Captain Abram Kean Jr., on the last ship to sail to the front* that year. On Saturday, March 15, they were near Horse Islands, north of the Baie Verte Peninsula, and came into exceptionally heavy ice. Captain Kean decided to burn down—that is, let the steamer's fires die down—and spend the night in a polynya.* That evening some of the crew and filmmakers sat around the red-hot bogey* in the saloon and drank tea while they yarned. Cabot persisted in whining uneasily beneath the table, and Henry Sargent, one of the Americans, patted him and attempted to put him at ease.

In Earl Pilgrim's highly fictionalized account of the episode in his recent book *The Day of Varrick Frissell*, Cabot is portrayed as a hero. In truth, poor Cabot had no chance to be a hero. Frissell, concerned because of the explosives on board, was busy making a warning sign using a piece of cardboard: P-O-W-D -. The Newfoundlanders thought it was funny, as every ship carried powder, dynamite, and cases of ammunition to the ice. The sign was never finished; around nine o'clock, *Viking*'s ice claw* broke free and the ship drifted across the open water to strike heavily upon the edge of the ice on the far side. The bogey* tipped over and the ensuing explosion killed twenty-seven, including Frissell, his cameraman, and the stalwart Cabot. More than a hundred survived to relate the horrific events.

Some dogs seem to have a premonition of the death of someone close to them. In one recent case a dog not only had the premonition, but did something about it. The *Winnipeg Sun* carried the story headlined, "Dog with X-ray vision saves dying man," on May 24, 2002, which is about as good a headline as could be written—without X-ray vision, how on earth did the dog know what was happening? Big Ben, or Benny, a nine-year-old Newfoundland living in Lac Dubonnet, Manitoba, was credited with saving the life of a neighbour. He ran to the man's porch and whined at the door to draw attention to a life-threatening situation. Inside, fifty-four-year-old Les Carlson, who lives alone, had slipped into diabetic shock and was critically in need of assistance. The *Sun* reported that early Monday evening, May 24, Benny, who seldom left the side of his guardian Eleanor Hladki, suddenly trotted away, whining.

"All of a sudden I could hear Benny crying," said Hladki. "He was on Les' deck. I went over to look at him and I thought he [Benny] was sick because he is getting on. But he was just crying and looking at Les' door." Hladki said she went inside and found Carlson lying unresponsive on the couch with his eyes glazed. An ambulance was called and he was rushed to the hospital from which, twenty-four hours later, he was released in good condition.

Carlson said if it weren't for Big Ben, "I wouldn't be here talking about it right now."

No one can explain how the dog sensed the man's grave condition. Although it has been extensively documented that dogs can detect low blood sugar in humans, researchers are at a loss to explain the phenomenon.

Another Neptune was also a dog with an apparent sixth sense. Clara Ramsey, a young woman in the late nineteenth century, and her husband lived on an isolated farm in New Hampshire. At home alone on Christmas Eve, her husband and children having gone to town, she was startled to hear someone cry, "Merry Christmas!" from the kitchen door.

There stood an unkempt stranger, but she was not particularly worried, as 150-pound Neptune was beside her. Mustering her courage she was about to order the tramp to leave when, to her surprise, Neptune took a loaf of freshly baked bread from the table and, with the air of greeting an old friend, took it to the obviously hungry man.

Feeling a little ashamed, she asked the man to step into the kitchen. He told her he had come from a schooner lost off Cape Porpoise at Kennebunkport, Maine, and was hiking back to his family's home in northern Vermont for Christmas. He patted the dog and told Ramsey, "We had a Newfoundland big as him, on our schooner."

Because of her trusted dog's attitude, Ramsey believed the man was what he claimed to be and apologized for her rudeness. She welcomed the cold and hungry sailor into her kitchen and set a substantial meal before him. While the man was eating, the dog suddenly barked and scratched at the door in an attempt to get out. The man jumped to his feet and ran outside, followed by Ramsey. To their horror, a terrific eruption of smoke, flame, and cinders was belching from the chimney.

The Newfoundland has an unmistakable air of insight.

The visitor grabbed a nearby ladder and mounted it with a bucket of water; once on the roof, he extinguished the fire in seconds. Ramsey's husband came home soon after the fire was put out and commented, "If it had not been for Neptune and his sailor friend, there would have been no Christmas for us." He later commented, "You know, that Neptune was the best guard dog we ever had. Funny how a Newfoundland knows an honest man."

The same sixth sense that alerts the Newfoundland to humans in trouble apparently applies to animals needing help as well. A dog from Sweetbay's Newfoundlands of Sherwood, Oregon, lived next door to a breeder of the famous Morgan horses. One day the dog set up a tremendous uproar and, when the rancher came to see what the fuss was all about, insisted that he follow him to the paddock. The man was in time to rescue a newborn foal that had stumbled headlong into a watering trough and was nearly drowned.

Of course, the sixth sense is not completely infallible. Sometimes the rescuer overwhelms the subject of this intuition and Newfoundland dogs save those who don't need their help. Ten-year-old Aaron had difficulty learning to swim, as each time he ventured into water up past his knees he was rescued by Boatswain, who could not fathom his suicidal bent (Mommm! Make him stop!). Nevertheless, this is a minor glitch in what is otherwise the remarkable ability of a Newfoundland to sniff out danger, and prevent it whenever possible.

Chapter 8

Along the Landwash

Formidable storms assault the Newfoundland coast, hammering the shore with waves that gouge solid rock and suck at the sand until it is pulled out into deep water. It's an environment that has given abundant opportunities for rescuers to engage in their line of work. For many decades, legends have been told of Newfoundland dogs. Their instinct for water and retrieving gives them an immense advantage over all other canines and makes them the dog for the long waterfront of sea, rivers, and lakes of North America.

In 1779, naturalist and engraver Sir Thomas Bewick was the first to make a point of the dog's webbed feet, and this characteristic in any other dog can be traced to its Newfoundland ancestry. Swimming in cold water comes naturally to Newfoundlands, and they tend to float higher in the water than other dogs. They swim not with a dog paddle, but a sort of breast-stroke—a smooth, effective motion in which their forelegs sweep out to the side more than other dogs' do. If you pay attention you'll notice a swimming Newfoundland has the inborn ability to handle waves, riptides, and currents that would baffle a human. Instead of fighting the water, the dog works with it, saving his energy. Their abilities make them one of the finest performers in the AKC and the CKC water trials.

Over the centuries it has been a combination of the dogs' skill in the water and their the dogs' devotion to people that has made them heroes. The plucky breed is credited for pulling so many people in distress from the water that it has earned the nickname "lifeguard dog." Following an instinctive urge to rescue people, a Newfoundland uses long, powerful strokes to reach someone in trouble, grasps a convenient portion of the potential victim in its large mouth, and drags him or her to safety.

A verse reflecting the Newfoundland's penchant for rescue work was written by Althea Bonnea and may be found in the *Dictionary of Dogs*:

> When featuring a dog review,
> Much laudatory praise is due,
> The Newfoundland—a dog world famed,
> That came from a small island named.
> A massive body, square-set thighs,
> A noble head and kindly eyes;
> A coast guard dog, it knows no fear,
> And oft saves lives when death is near.

The Newfoundland, in effecting a rescue, has a sense of priorities that usually runs like this: baby, child, woman, then man. Even Newfoundlands who for some reason don't naturally like the water become wonderful lifesavers.

By the mid-1700s the Newfoundland was seeing action in many parts of the world. In 1746, Reverend W. B. Bezanson's *Stories of Acadia* contained the tale of Joe Copee, a Mi'kmaq, presumably living in Nova Scotia. He had a camp near a ford across an unnamed river, that he and his family shared with their Newfoundland dog, Duc. Their neighbours were Paul Labrador and his wife and three

Sir Edwin Henry Landseer's late–eighteenth century painting *Saved* shows the breed's propensity for water rescue.

children, who had a farm on a narrow-necked peninsula.

At midwinter an unusually warm spell brought the river to an unheard-of level, and water and ice flowed over the isthmus of Labrador's land, surrounding his farm. Fearing the entire peninsula might become submerged, Copee sent Duc across the river to the marooned family. Duc quickly returned with the youngest of the Labrador children tied on his back. Two more trips and the children were safe, then the dog went back carrying a lifeline. Labrador fastened the line to a toboggan on which his wife sat, and Copee pulled her across, then Labrador was brought over in a similar manner.

Many a seafarer had a useful Newfoundland dog, but so did many landlubbers. A ship en route from North America to Great Britain, around 1790, went on the rocks of a small isolated island. While the crew and passengers managed to get to solid ground, they had no food whatsoever. The captain reported that they survived because of the industriousness and sagacity of a Newfoundland owned by one of the passengers, believed to be a British man, General Proctor. For more than a month and a half, they survived on rations of salt pork that the dog salvaged, regularly searching the frigid waters for such flotsam. A decade later the same General Proctor was sent to Ontario, with another Newfoundland, Neptune, with whom we'll deal a little further on.

Many years ago a William Phillips was bathing at Portsmouth, England, and ventured out too far. Caught in the current and rapidly tiring, he was in imminent peril of drowning. Amazingly, two men in a boat, instead of going to his rescue, greedily attempted to strike a bargain with onlookers who had pressed them to go to the man's aid. While this fiduciary discussion took place, a Newfoundland, seeing the struggling swimmer, plunged into the water and pulled him to safety.

To Phillips' credit he found his rescuer's owner, a butcher, and bought the dog. For the rest of the dog's life Phillips held a yearly festival at which his friend was given the place of honour and a good allotment of steak. He had a portrait of his dog painted by George Morland, well known for his works depicting animals, then had an engraving made by the equally famous Francesco Bartolozzi. He had the resultant picture worked into all his table linen and below it the motto *Virum extuli mari*, "heroic rescuer of the sea."

Lieutenant Edward Chappell, captain of sloop-of-war HMS *Rosamond*, came to Newfoundland in 1813, when he was twenty-one. He noted in his book, *Voyage of his Majesty's Ship Rosamond to Newfoundland and the Southern Coast of Labrador* (1818), that Newfoundland dogs: "will leap from the summit of the highest cliff into the water in obedience to the commands of their master."

Though Patrick O'Flaherty notes in his book *The Rock Observed* that Chappell is not be trusted on any subject, Harold MacPherson reported that he had witnessed the dogs diving to a depth of ten feet (three metres) to retrieve a stone, and that from a bridge twelve feet (three-and-a-half metres) above the water. In another case a

Newfoundland commonly leapt from a dock eight feet (two metres) above the water to a depth of twelve feet or more, to retrieve objects thrown there for his entertainment.

MacPherson's Oscar, whom he raised in the early 1900s, could swim underwater for an astonishingly long time, and beneath the ice for that matter. And as for their ability to handle cold water, one modern-day Boatswain (the author's first Newfoundland dog) made a practice of wading along ditches cracking the half-inch-thick ice between his jaws as he went.

There has been much debate regarding the accuracy of the following tales about Hairy Man and Watch, regarding both the dogs' names and the different dates given for the incident. Nevertheless, the stories are excellent examples of the Newfoundland's usefulness along the landwash. The first story involves the English emigrant brig *Despatch*, bound for Quebec from Liverpool with between 150 and 180 passengers and crew (this figure is as much in dispute as the rest of the story).

On July 12, 1828, while attempting to round Cape Ray in a tremendous gale, *Despatch* struck Wreck Rock at Seal Cove, three miles (five kilometres) from the home of George Harvey, an Isle-aux-Morts fisherman. Harvey heard the distress signals and immediately launched his boat. With his twelve-year-old son, Tom, seventeen-year-old daughter, Ann, and Hairy Man, he tried to reach the wreck.

Those on the doomed ship crowded onto the forecastle, in imminent peril. The sea raged between Harvey's boat and the wreck, but the fisherman and his children pushed their frail skiff across the waste of water. To get close to the stranded vessel was to court instant destruction and saving those on board seemed out of the question; however, Hairy Man, an intelligent dog and a bold swimmer, seemed to understand what was required of him. At a signal from Harvey he sprang from the boat and swam for the ship. The seas overwhelmed him and drove him under many times; nevertheless, he persevered, and finally came near enough to catch a line bent* to a belaying pin that the sailors threw him. He at last got back to his master, gripping the line in his teeth, and was drawn into the boat, nearly dead from exhaustion.

Harvey anchored the line on shore and, with the most laborious efforts, all were saved. King George IV was so pleased with Harvey's exploit that he gave him, through Newfoundland's Governor Cochrane, one hundred sovereigns, a large gold medal especially engraved with a description of his deed, and a personally signed letter.

Ten years later, on September 14, 1838, Harvey saved the twenty-five man crew of the *Rankin*, a ship owned by a wealthy Glaswegian. *Rankin* went to pieces and the crew were hanging onto the rail around the poop, when in the same fearless manner Harvey and his team— now with a different dog, Watch—brought them off in safety.

For years afterward any ships passing within hearing range of the Harvey home sounded their horns in salute. The Harveys and their dogs were thus immortalized, at least in Newfoundland, for these episodes. Today, the "Newfoundland dog sign" on Harvey's Trail commemorates the events.

Bob was the dog honoured by Landseer's celebrated painting *A Distinguished Member of the Humane Society*, for which Paul Pry served as model. Shipwrecked twice, he and his master once swam two miles to safety, but the second time his master drowned. Bob made his way to London and became something of a celebrity, though not a great deal is now known of him save for the fact that, in typical Newfoundland fashion, he saved at least twenty-three lives in his fourteen-year career on the London waterfront. He was adopted by the Royal Humane Society and awarded a special collar with a gold medal and a special commission to save lives. Certainly, he was one of the great dogs of all time.

In 1856, *Emma*, a 207-ton brig owned by Bowrings of St. John's and Liverpool, England, skippered by a Captain White, was on its way to St. John's with a cargo of salt. On November 5, thirty days out of Liverpool, the Newfoundland coast was visible and White realized they were farther north than he had planned. He had changed course for St. John's when, that evening, the wind died down leaving a heavy swell. Without the wind to claw offshore, his vessel was driven onto the rocks at Seal Cove, between Pouch Cove and Torbay. The crew made it to shore despite the heaving sea and the ferocious surf. Their Italian cook, considered a good swimmer, attempted to make it to shore, but he died when the waves smashed him on the rocks. The others managed to launch the brig's boat and eventually thrashed their way to shore, landing in a small gully. Here, to their consternation, they found they were unable to climb the vertical seventy-foot (twenty-one-metre) cliffs that stood before them.

It was a very cold night and the half-frozen men shouted in desperation, hoping that they might be heard. A dog barked a response and they considered that to mean someone lived in the vicinity. They were worried when the barking stopped; nevertheless, they had been heard by a benefactor. A Newfoundland dog, owned by a fisherman named Mayo, had heard them and felt that someone was in difficulty. He raced home and scratched at the door until Mayo answered it. Concerned by the dog's unusual actions, he thought that something must be wrong and called to his sons to get dressed.

The three followed the dog to the cliff and discovered the men stranded below. Neighbours were roused and in a short time ropes were being let down to the *Emma*'s crew. The ascent was made before daybreak, and shortly afterward their vessel went to pieces and was driven out to sea. The crew then walked across country and arrived in the Bowrings' office at St. John's to acquaint them with the loss of their vessel and its cargo.

It seems the only picture of Charles Kress' Romey, a hero of Pennsylvania's Johnstown Flood of 1889, is a stereogram of the solemn Newfoundland dog sitting on a front step, a young girl beside him with her arm around his shoulders. The girl is leaning on a man with a cigar clamped between his teeth. The August 1, 1998, edition of *The Birmingham Post* reported the story of his heroism.

On May 31, 1889, heavy rains caused a poorly engineered reservoir dam, twelve miles (nineteen kilometres) upstream from the city, to give way. The resulting flood submerged Johnstown and caused between two and three thousand deaths.

The Kress family, who had taken refuge on the slippery roof of their Washington Street home, suddenly felt the house lurch beneath them. Mrs. Kress, a maid, and a child were precipitated into the murky floodwaters below. Without an instant's hesitation Romey threw himself into the water and pulled each to safety on a lower portion of the roof.

In 1897 Mr. A. A. Martin of New London, Connecticut, was hunting from a rowboat on the James River above Richmond, Virginia, accompanied by Colored Boy, his Newfoundland. Suddenly, a cry for help sliced through the silence, and as if on command the dog bounded over the side of the boat and swam to a man who was obviously in difficulty. Grasping the man's coat, the dog towed him to shore, then dragged him from the water.

After the man, a Mr. Jenkins, had regained his senses he asked Martin to sell the dog to him. Martin refused, but Jenkins pressed him numerous times in an effort to obtain ownership of his rescuer. Jenkins died a few years later and bequeathed two thousand dollars and other property to the dog and his owner, who travelled together to Virginia to take delivery of the inheritance.

At Bareneed, on the southwest side of Conception Bay, Newfoundland, young Wilf Richards was on the wharf watching fishermen securing their boats during a storm. Somehow, he tumbled from the wharf into the deep roiling waters. With no boats near enough to help he faced certain drowning, but Dan, Jacob Bartlett's Newfoundland, heard his cries and plummeted from the wharf to the boy's aid. The dog dragged the apparently lifeless boy to shore where Aunt Lily Bartlett "rolled him over a barrel"—placed his body over a barrel and rolled it back and forth to expel the water, as was common practice—and revived him.

Another Newfoundland showed up in the nick of time near Kent, England, when a ship went onto the rocks at Lydd. The crew of eight seemed doomed when the lifeboat could not be launched in the churning surf. The dog, accompanied by his owner, arrived on the scene and the man, pointing out the ship, gave his friend a short stick. The dog appeared to understand completely and bounded into the water. Battling the wind-whipped water he approached the ship but, with the waves breaking over it and the rocks, he couldn't get close enough to deliver his burden. The crew understood the meaning of the stick and tied a light messenger line to another and flung it far out, enabling the dog to grasp it.

He struck out powerfully and unfalteringly for the shore, vanishing time and time again in the surf, until he reached the beach and his master. Those on shore fastened a heavier line to this messenger and the imperiled crew pulled it out and secured it to the ship. All eight men struggled to shore and safety, along the line.

Ben More and his dog Justice stumbled upon yet another life-or-death drama in England. The June 1997 edition of *Downhome* reports that while walking on the common at Bournemouth, a town near Poole in Dorset, England, they heard a woman cry for help. They didn't have to search too long before they found twenty-one-year-old Vicky O'Brien up to her neck in mud and water, clinging to a tree branch.

More waded into the bog to help, but was still too far to rescue her when his dog plunged in. Despite being partially crippled and unable to use one of his hind legs, the intrepid dog succeeded in reaching the woman, who grabbed his collar and was pulled to safety.

Vicky, who stepped into the bog after her nephew's Staffordshire bull terrier puppy ran away, is convinced she would have died but for Justice.

"Every time I tried to move my legs, I went in farther," she said. "I couldn't see any way out of there. It was late in the day and I didn't think anybody was going to come along."

She rewarded Justice with a large bone and some doggy treats and said she would never forget her wonderful rescuer.

A news item in the St. John's *Daily News* on June 28, 1928, told the story of another life saved by one of our dogs, Jumbo. This time it was in Prowseton, a resettled* fishing community on the west side of Placentia Bay:

> John Walter Gibbons, son of J. Gibbons, postal operator of Prowsetown [sic], had a narrow escape from drowning: whilst the boy was fishing for tom cods, he tripped and fell head first into the deep water. A large Newfoundland Dog named Jumbo, owned by Patrick Hickey, saw the boy, jumped overboard and swam to him. The boy caught hold of the dog and held fast and the noble animal took him to land. The little fellow was in an exhausted condition, but after a short while was none the worse for the experience. The dog is a hero and deserves a medal.

Often a Newfoundland dog is not as avid a swimmer as you might imagine and needs a good reason to go into the water. Harold MacPherson writes in the first volume of *The Book of Newfoundland* that when one of his dogs, Billy, was ten months old, he was taken along by a group who went to swim in the ocean. They failed to coax him into the waves but when MacPherson swam out some distance, yelled for help, then threw up his arms and sank, Billy howled and immediately rushed to his aid. He never again showed any reluctance to enter the water.

In Swansea, southern Wales, the city's namesake Swansea Jack, as he was affectionately known, rescued at least twenty-seven humans and two dogs during his career. Most of his actions took place during the 1930s along the waterfront of the port and the rugged seacliffs of the area. He patrolled the quays and at the first sound of a splash and a cry lunged into the water and swiftly swam to the rescue. Unfortunately, despite his splendid record nothing more seems to be known of this great dog.

Johnny, a young Newfoundland, spent his first summer with his family holidaying at Branford, near New Haven, Connecticut, on Long Island Sound. He accompanied the neighbourhood children to the beach, where he swam and played with them. Usually he swam out to a raft where he was in a position to watch his friends. When, in his opinion, a child's swimming ability was in doubt, Johnny went into action. Diving from the raft he hastily dragged the "imperilled," and often indignant, child to shore.

In March 2004, Melvin Dawe of Sandy Cove, Bonavista Bay, told of Nelson, whom he met at Harbour Grace in 1948 while his ship was in dry dock. A delivery truck pulled up at a nearby building, and while the driver was inside, a small child crawled beneath his vehicle. Nelson became aware of a problem when the driver emerged and started for the truck. The vigilant dog hurried to the truck and inched his way underneath until he could get a grip on the child's clothing, then backed out, dragging the protesting youngster. Evidently, no one but the sailors and dockworkers were aware of Nelson's action—certainly not the child's parents or the driver.

The Lifeguard by Edwin Megargee, from the early twentieth century, is a good example of the widespread—and well-founded—believe in the dogs' lifesaving abilities.

A German visiting Holland with his Newfoundland dog was ambling along a dyke when he lost his footing and fell into the water. Not being a swimmer, he sank, after some preliminary thrashing around, and lost consciousness. When he came to his senses he was in a house amid the concerned people who had found and revived him.

One of them told of seeing his big dog labouring to get something to shore. The steep sides of the dyke prevented him from landing just anywhere, but at long last the dog reached a stream and got his burden onto the grass. Here they found him gently licking his master's face.

The Newfoundland had attempted to keep the man's head above water while holding him by the shoulder and, failing that, he had changed his grip to the back his neck. The dog had swum, pushing and pulling the man, more than five hundred yards (450 metres) before he found a stream, on the opposite side of the canal, where the bank was low enough for him to pull the man onto solid ground. The man had a large bruise on the nape of his neck and another on his shoulder, but that's much better than breathing canal water.

In 1995 Boo and his owner, Lillian, were walking along the Yuba River in northern California. As they came around a sharp bend, the ten-month-old dog spotted trouble. Without hesitation he dove into the water and swam toward a man who was clinging to a red gas can, desperately trying to stay afloat in the swollen stream. Boo grabbed the man's arm and with some difficulty pulled him safely to shore.

"Boo had no training in water rescue," explained Janice Anderson on the Discovery Channel's August 13, 2000, broadcast of *Animal Heroes*. Anderson is a Newfoundland breeder of thirty years from whose kennels Boo had come. She identified the man as Link Hill, a deaf mute who had fallen from a gold dredge and couldn't call for help. "It was just instinct. [Boo] picked up on the fact that there was someone in distress and then dealt with the situation."

The next year, the Newfoundland Club of America, in Cheyenne, Wyoming, presented Boo with a medal for his life-saving action. Peggy Lynde, of Long Beach, California, trains Newfoundland dogs to go to the aid of surfers and swimmers in distress. Nicky, one of her dogs (and Boo's cousin), reenacted the heroic deed on the Discovery Channel in 1998.

Another extraordinary dog lived along the landwash near the end of the nineteenth century. This sea rescue performed by a landlubbing dog near Pigeon Cove begins with a mystery: which Pigeon Cove? There's a Pigeon Cove near St. Barbe at the top end of the Great Northern Peninsula, another north of Cape Dégrat on Quirpon Island, one halfway between Williamsport and Great Harbour Deep on the east side of the same peninsula, and yet another about twelve miles (nineteen kilometres) from Trepassey. There may have been others, but the most likely location of the incident is at the cove near Trepassey. The outcome of the tragedy is also unresolved, but it seems likely that only two men were saved.

In any case, the story of the daring rescue by someone's Newfoundland dog, likely in the late nineteenth century, reads:

> About twelve o'clock the mainmast gave way. At that time there were on the main-top and shrouds about thirty persons. By the fall of the mast the whole of these unhappy wretches were plunged into the water and ten only regained the top-mast which rested on the main yard and the whole remained fast to the foundering ship by some of the rigging. Of the ten who thus reached the topmast, four only were alive when morning appeared. Nine were at that time alive on the mizzen, but three were so exhausted and so helpless that they were washed away before any relief arrived; two others perished, and thus only four were at last left alive on the mizzen.
>
> At the place where the ship went down it was barely a hundred fathoms* to the east of the entrance of Pigeon Cove. Some fishermen came down in the night to the point

opposite to which the ship foundered, kept up large fires on the shore, and were so near that their shouts could be heard by the crew on board the wreck. The first exertion that was made for their relief was by a powerful Newfoundland dog from Pigeon Cove who ventured out to the wreck bearing a line in his teeth. This dog with great labour and risk to himself boldly approached the wreck and maneuvered amid the breaking seas so close to the mizzen-top as to pass the line to the two men who could not with safety hold on any more.

Many shipwrecked sailors and clumsy swimmers have been lucky to be rescued by a Newfoundland dog, and there is no doubt that the dogs will continue to perform their heroic rescues along the landwash.

Chapter 9

Sea Dog

Within living memory nearly every fishing vessel—
Newfoundland-owned or not—carried a Newfoundland dog
if it could. Not only were they an aid in hauling nets in the days before power winches, but if a man or any equipment went overboard,
the dog went over the side to fetch. Further, they were indispensable
navigational aids. As early as a day or two before a ship's lookout
sighted land, the dog would be aware of its general location. It would
stand in the prow, sniffing the breezes, and often the skipper would
steer according to the direction indicated by the dog.

Margaret Booth Chern tells the following tale in *The New Complete
Newfoundland.* A ship out of Newcastle was driven onto the rocks and
wrecked near Yarmouth, on Britain's Isle of Wight, during an intense
winter storm in 1799. A Newfoundland dog who managed to fight
his way to shore was the sole survivor. Although he saved no lives, he
did accomplish one thing. He identified the vessel that had been lost,
and thus those on board, by carrying the captain's "pocketbook," or
wallet, to the beach. After a cursory glance at those who had collected there, he decided to take his treasure to one specific man.

This accomplished, he went to the point on the beach closest to
the wreck and stood with his attention rivetted on it. He managed
to secure and bring to shore a piece of wreckage that floated in
and for days he remained at his self-appointed post. Eventually,

Lord Granville convinced the dog to come home with him, and the dog lived there for years. Granville named his new friend Tippo and, when the dog later died, he buried him at Dropmore, England, and wrote a Latin eulogy that was carved on his marble monument.

In 1816, the British transport HMS *Harpooner*, commanded by Captain Joseph Briant, was en route to Deptford, England, from Quebec. On board were soldiers and their families returning home after the War of 1812. On November 10, *Harpooner* ran ashore in Marine Cove at Eastern Head near St. Shotts, on the southern tip of Newfoundland's Avalon Peninsula. It was smashed against the rocks and 208 of its 385 men, women, and children passengers were lost, as were an undetermined number of her crew. Were it not for the intelligence and courage of the captain's Newfoundland, many more would have died.

In a move that echoes the actions of so many noble dogs that live along the landwash, the seafaring dog was given a messenger line, and sprang into the furious, frigid water to fight his way to shore. Despite being smashed against the rocks and driven under by the surf and wind until he was half drowned, this tough and diligent animal enabled scores of passengers to reach land safely.

In another instance, a whaling schooner, believed to be the eighty-five-ton *William and Ann* out of St. John's, was on a Greenland voyage in 1830 when it chanced upon some men who had been on an iceberg, near their boat. The event was recorded thus by an unknown party:

Seven men were on an iceberg. It gave way. Six of them got hold of the bow-ropes, but the seventh sank. The waters closed over him, and his comrades concluded he was lost. Mr. Smith, master of the whaler, was in bed at the time, but hearing the noise, he promptly sprang on deck, and, in obedience to his signal, boats from the other vessels immediately came to assistance.

His faithful Newfoundland was at his feet, and gazing intently, he observed the head of the sailor above the water. He pointed it out—gave the word—the dog leaped from the bow of the vessel, and while swimming towards the man, he barked, either with anxiety, or with a view to cheer the perishing sailor with the prospect of assistance. When the dog was within a few feet of his objective, the drowning man was picked up in a state of utter insensibility by a boat from the *Rambler* of Kirkcaldy [Scotland]. Observing the rescue, the dog returned to his own ship, and when taken on board, his gambols, frisking and fawning on his master indicated that though he had not saved the man, he was aware that he had gone to his aid and the sailor was safe.

—from Booth Chern, *The New Complete Newfoundland*

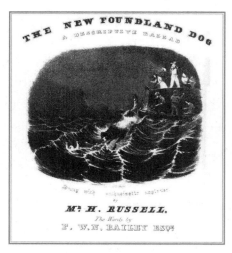

The songsheet for *The Newfoundland Dog,* a ballad from around 1845, shows a daring at-sea rescue.

This next story may well be rated a fable by some, but it was related in the *British Workman* in the late nineteenth century as a true tale. It is well worth re-telling.

The brig *Cecilia* was commanded by a bad-tempered Captain Symmes, who had among his crew a man named Lancaster and his first-rate Newfoundland dog, Napoleon. The dog was remarkable for his magnificent size, proportions, and intelligence. The captain, however, harboured a dislike for animals of any kind and had an un-accountable hatred of dogs. This dislike was shockingly manifested one day when Napoleon entered the captain's cabin and his great tail knocked paper and ink off the desk. This was the second time it had happened, and Symmes grabbed a knife and slashed off part of the poor dog's tail. The aggrieved dog's yelp brought Lancaster, who, seeing what had happened, dropped the captain to the deck with one punch to his head. Lancaster was immediately put in irons but after a cooling of tempers he was released. Symmes was sorry for his cruel and rash action, especially after he learned that Napoleon had once saved his owner's life.

Napoleon wasn't reticent in showing his displeasure whenever the captain approached and, fearful for the dog's life, Lancaster tried to curb these signs of hatred. However, Symmes made allowances for it and left the dog alone.

A few weeks later, with the *Cecilia* running at fifteen knots, the cry, "Man overboard!" was raised. The captain, standing on the bowsprit, had lost his footing and slipped into the sea. White sharks swam in these waters and there was a rush to launch a boat, but by the time the boat was in the water their worst fears were realized: a short distance from the swimmer a fin protruded from the water.

At the beginning of the commotion Napoleon growled, then this changed to whines. Suddenly, there was a splash as the big dog hit the water. He rapidly made his way to the nearly exhausted captain while the shark closed in. The ship's boat was following the dog, but before it could overtake him the shark rolled onto its back for the attack. The captain screamed and Napoleon, with a burst of energy and a fierce growl, buried his teeth in the shark's shining belly. The boat was nearly upon them now, but Napoleon retained his grip and was dragged under as the shark rolled again.

Lancaster, knife between his teeth, plunged in where the captain had by now sunk from view. A moment later the dog appeared on the surface, followed by Lancaster with the insensible captain. The shark rushed in again but was foiled by the men in the boat slapping oars on the water in front of it. Again the shark attacked, barely missing the captain's leg as they dragged him into the boat. The big fish finally disappeared leaving a trail of blood, a sign of the severity of its wound.

A short while after returning to the brig, the embarrassed captain appeared on deck, weak but appreciative of his canine saviour.

"I would give my right arm," he said, as he patted the dog, "if I could only repair the injury I have done this splendid fellow. Lancaster you are avenged, and a most Christian vengeance it is, though it will be a source of grief to me as long as I live."

As an aside, a great white shark was caught off Australia some years ago and scientists listed among the contents of its stomach a Newfoundland dog. So, no need to feel sorry for the shark.

Buller was another seagoing dog, and a three-family dog at that. Andrew Horwood writes of him in *Dogs That Were No Fiction*. The only time Buller acknowledged any of the three families to be more important than another was when it came time for the floaters* to go on the Labrador fishery. Only one family went fishing and Buller refused to be left out of that. He knew the routine on board the schooner and fit himself into it perfectly.

He kept his own watch and knew the routes to Labrador and its harbours so well that he could have been a pilot. When a familiar piece of land came in sight, he barked happily. The skipper had great faith in Buller's ability to select a good trap-berth.

Another Newfoundland was present on September 22, 1866, at 5:00 p.m., when a storm occurred that lived long in the memories of the inhabitants of St. Pierre. In a three-hour period there was tremendous damage and loss of life as both the port and the anchorage in the roadstead were crowded with vessels newly returned from the fishing season.

When the gale struck, many ships dragged their anchors, colliding with their neighbours. In the roadstead the French troop transport *L'Abondance* parted its anchor chain and was thrown into the breakers. At 2:00 a.m. it sank, leaving only its masts sticking out of the water. All but three of its crew escaped and the pluck and ability of a Newfoundland dog was recorded as instrumental in saving their lives. As in countless other stories, the ship's dog swam from his sinking vessel through the raging waters, taking a line to shore that saved the crew's lives.

In *Newfoundland Ships and Men,* Andrew Horwood tells the amazing tale of a true sea dog, who belonged to John Hillier of Hants Harbour, Trinity Bay. Hillier was the owner and skipper of a Labrador schooner, the forty-three-ton *Myra*, on which he, his dog, and his crew lived for the entire summer fishing season.

For business reasons Hillier moved to Twillingate, and in 1899 he returned from Labrador with his catch. As usual he sought out coasting* voyages to eke out his summer's earnings, and merchant William Ashbourne, his supplier, arranged for him to bring a cargo of winter merchandise from St. John's to Twillingate.

Four days before Christmas the *Myra*, with its captain and crew of four, left St. John's. They spent the night at Catalina and the next day continued on their way. They were making good progress when, as they were crossing Gander Bay, a sudden squall struck and snapped both masts.

The schooner *Spectator*, skippered by a Captain Willis, was nearby and came through the blow without damage. Willis brought his vessel alongside the *Myra* and offered to take its crew off and leave the damaged schooner to its fate. However, Hillier wanted to save his ship and cargo and said that if he had help he could bring them to a safe anchorage. He asked for volunteers but they were a scarce commodity; indeed, they tried to persuade him to leave the *Myra* and save his life.

The *Spectator* took the crew and sailed away, leaving Hillier and his Newfoundland dog to save the vessel or go with it to the bottom. It took Hillier longer than he had hoped to rig jury masts and to set small sails, and before he could complete the job, land was out of sight, with the *Myra* drifting southeast. It was not a new vessel and had soon begun to take water so that, between pumping and rigging, Hillier had little time for anything else and it's amazing he accomplished what he did.

From his position at the wheel the captain had no view of what lay ahead, but his dog seemed to sense the problem and kept a sharp lookout. Whether it was his sense of smell or some means beyond human ken that told him where land was, he always looked in the right direction. They had been drifting for three days when the dog let it be known that they were nearing the shore. As soon as he saw the point of land he barked until the skipper left the wheel, went forward, and identified Cape Bonavista.

A 1920s postcard depicting Harold MacPherson's Westerland Watch.

After that it was easy. The vessel was brought into Catalina again and Hillier wired Ashbourne to explain that he would be late for his Christmas trade. The four men who had been taken off the ship were somewhat reluctant to discuss the affair, but Hillier bore no grudge and made light of the incident. He also declared that he would never sail again without the company of a Newfoundland dog to stand steadfastly by his side.

On July 21, 1903, a dreadful storm burst at the southern tip of the Avalon Peninsula. Nine miles (fourteen-and-a-half kilometres) off Cape Pine, Burin merchant Charles F. Bishop's fifty-two-ton schooner *Nightingale* fought for its life. Amidst the roar of confused water and wind, Thomas Deer and John Isaacs were attempting to reduce sail when a sudden gust and a lurch sent them both over the taffrail.*

The chance of survival was slight as the schooner had great difficulty in heaving to and launching a boat to attempt a rescue. At once, the schooner's Newfoundland dog leapt into the water and, with powerful strokes, made it to Isaacs' side and grasped his collar. The dog struggled to keep him afloat for the long minutes it took to stop the progress of the schooner and launch the dory, then he fought his way to the dory's side with his burden. Deer had disappeared almost immediately and was never seen again; ironically, Isaacs drowned a few years later.

Near the end of the nineteenth century a French brigantine, *La Marie*, ran into an autumn gale and began losing spars and canvas to such an extent that it was unmanageable. Its seams opened, and even with the crew pumping round the clock it couldn't live much longer in those seas. Foundering, it was at last sighted by the SS *Muldeau*, which steamed in so as to put the labouring brigantine under its lee. With the protection of the steamer, the French crew were launching their boats when a tremendous wave washed over their vessel. Confusion reigned and one man was washed overboard.

Straight away, the ship's Newfoundland dog sprang to his aid and grasped the man's collar, holding his head out of the water. In the raging wind the crew managed to bring a boat about and fight their way to their shipmate and hauled him and the dog into it. The pleased rescuer gracefully accepted the adulation of the crew, who praised and petted him, as was his just due.

Sometimes derided as a myth, this next story has been printed as fact in many publications and is presented here as such. It seems that three dogs survived the sinking of the *Titanic* in 1912, and although two escaped in lifeboats, one was a hero. A Pomeranian owned by Miss Margaret Hays of New York and a Pekinese owned by Henry Sleeper Harper of the publishing family boarded early lifeboats in the arms of their owners. The boats were so empty that no one complained.

The hero of the disaster was Rigel, a big black Newfoundland owned by *Titanic's* First Officer William Murdoch. The dog spent more than three hours searching for his master in waters of twenty-eight degrees Fahrenheit (two degrees Celsius). The following is an account of the event as it appeared in the *New York Herald* on Sunday, April 21, 1912:

> Lieutenant William McMaster Murdoch, Dalbeattie in Scotland, the First Officer of the White Star super-liner RMS *Titanic* and the owner of Rigel. Not the least among the heroes of the Titanic was Rigel, a big black Newfoundland dog, belonging to the first officer, who went down with his ship. But for Rigel, the fourth boat picked up might have been run down by the *Carpathia*. For three hours he swam in the water where the Titanic went down, evidently looking for his master, and was instrumental in guiding the boatload of survivors to the gangway of the *Carpathia*.
>
> Jonas Briggs, a seaman aboard the *Carpathia,* now has Rigel and told the story of the dog's heroism. The *Carpathia* was moving slowly about, looking for boats, rafts or anything which might be afloat. Exhausted with their efforts, weak from lack of food and exposure to the cutting wind, and terror stricken, the men and woman in the fourth boat drifted under the *Carpathia's* starboard bow. They were dangerously close to the steamship, too weak to shout a warning loud enough to reach the bridge.

The boat might not have been seen were it not for the sharp barking of Rigel, who was swimming ahead of the craft and valiantly announcing his position. The barks attracted the attention of Captain Rostron and he went to the starboard end of the bridge to see where they came from and saw the boat. He immediately ordered the engines stopped and the boat came alongside the starboard gangway.

Care was taken to take Rigel aboard, but he appeared little affected by his long trip through the ice cold water. He stood by the rail and barked until Captain Rostron called Briggs and had him take the dog below.

—quoted in Logan,
The Sinking of the Titanic & Great Sea Disasters

With the loss of Lieutenant Murdoch, Rigel was forced to adopt Briggs as his new and permanent master, a responsibility the latter gladly accepted.

It's not necessary to rescue someone or otherwise accomplish heroic deeds to be recognized as a real sea dog. Captain George "Ki" Noseworthy, of Fortune, on Newfoundland's Burin Peninsula, commanded the 205-ton rum-running tern schooner *Côte Nord* during Prohibition in the 1920s. His son Gordon tells Robert C. Parsons, author of *Committed to the Deep,* of an occasion when the *Côte Nord* was a mile off Long Beach, New York. The *Thorndyke* arrived and moored not too far from them.

Jack McCarty, of Bay St. George, a friend of Ki's and a fellow rum-runner, skippered the *Thorndyke* and had a big Newfoundland on board. The dog visited his friends on the *Côte Nord* regularly by jumping overboard and swimming to the other schooner. The crew would let down a line, he'd put his paws in the loop, and they'd haul him aboard. After a stay of two or three hours, he'd get up on the rail, jump over the side, and swim home to the *Thorndyke*, where the boarding process was repeated.

In mid-July 1927, the Canadian Custom Preventive Vessel *Bayfield* seized the fifty-seven-foot long, thirty-five-ton rum-running schooner *Nellie J. Banks* (about which Geoff and Dorothy Robinson wrote their book of the same name, which includes this tale), home of the aptly named ship's dog, Whisky. While the crew, resigned to their detainment, opened a keg of rum in the forecastle, Whisky insisted on taking his evening swim despite the protests of those who saw him going over the side.

He came close to being left behind when the *Bayfield* began towing his schooner away. The attempt to sail off without the dog so enraged the no-longer-sober crew that one man went so far as to partially cut the towline. The *Banks'* skipper, Burgeo's Captain Joe Vatcher, was summoned to get the situation under control. "Look boys, we're in trouble enough," he implored. *Bayfield*'s Captain McCarthy evaluated the situation and decided things would certainly get out of hand if the dog were to be left behind. Whisky was rescued and the journey to Pictou, Nova Scotia, continued.

The 392-ton tern* schooner *Flowerdew*, owned by Patten and Forsey of Grand Bank, was skippered by Captain James Bellman. On October 5, 1927, it sailed from Grand Turk, of the Turks and Caicos Islands in the West Indies, for Newfoundland with a load of salt.

Within a few days it began leaking, and the pumps were in continuous operation until the eleventh day, when salt, probably the most dangerous cargo carried by these vessels, clogged them. Bellman ordered cargo jettisoned and, fortunately, the big Italian liner *Benta II* appeared on the fourteenth. At 8:00 a.m. on the fifteenth the *Flowerdew*'s crew was forced to abandon their schooner, and it went to the bottom two hundred miles (320 kilometres) off Savannah, Georgia. When Captain Bellman and his crew were taken on board the *Bentall*, he took with him his Newfoundland puppy.

Captain Nicolo Gaidrossich, master of the liner, was so taken with the puppy that, in gratitude for the rescue, Bellman gave it to him. The Italian was thrilled with the gift and thought it more than compensated him for his act of humanity.

One of the most impressive feats of heroism and determination of a dog ever recorded occurred on the night of October 26, 1932. P. J. Wakeham tells a compelling version of the story in the Fall 1990 edition of *New-Land Magazine*. The twenty-five-ton schooner *Mary Ryan* of Great Paradise, Placentia Bay, was returning from St. Pierre with a cargo of contraband. Rum-running was profitable and those who sailed the vessels often took great risks in attempting to elude the law.

The ship left port around 6:00 p.m. with a brisk westerly wind speeding it along. Running without lights through the clear, moonless night, it was sailing nicely and Captain Ryan gave the man on watch with him permission to go to the forecastle for a midnight meal. At the time, they were off Cape Chapeau Rouge and the rest of the crew were sleeping, but Skipper, Ryan's Newfoundland dog, was on watch.

The man below had just begun eating when the schooner lurched and the canvas flapped loudly as though it had been put in stays.*

Hurrying up the companionway, the man called to the captain but received no reply. When he reached the deck, he found that Captain Ryan and Skipper had vanished.

Correctly assuming the captain had fallen overboard and that Skipper had gone to his rescue, the roused crew hove to. Though the captain couldn't swim, a few of the crew felt that Skipper could keep him afloat for some time, as he was a particularly large and powerful dog. Their greatest concern was that they might run down the man and dog in the darkness. In minutes they had their dory in the water with two men in it and with a lantern mounted in the bow. Another man clambered out onto the bowsprit of the schooner with a lantern on a rope, and this he lowered to within a yard of the waves. The lights would let the captain know they were searching and might even give him a point to aim for.

The sea was rough, and knowing where to search in the darkness was difficult. The wind diminished, but as each hour passed, concern grew. Still, the mate asserted that Skipper was rugged enough to keep the captain afloat and that they would remain in the area and search until daylight.

Day was breaking when the discouraged men in the dory heard Skipper bark. To windward, whenever the dory rose on the crest of a wave, they saw something in the water. It took what seemed like hours to reach the area, and, when they arrived there, to their astonishment they found Skipper still holding Ryan's head above water. They canted the dory over and dragged the exhausted pair into it.

The crew made a great fuss over Skipper while Captain Ryan described his misadventure. The schooner was running before the wind when it "boomed out," the foresail taking the wind on one side and the mainsail on the other. When the mainsail suddenly swung over, the boom hit him a terrific blow, throwing him into the sea. He concluded that Skipper had come to his rescue immediately for, when he recovered his senses the big dog had him by the shoulder, thus holding his head above water. Captain Ryan's greatest fear, that of Skipper becoming tired and releasing his grip, was unrealized. He kept one arm around the dog's neck in the event he did lose his hold, but the only time Skipper let go was when he barked to attract the attention of their rescuers. He instantly regained his hold and maintained it until the men in the dory pulled them in.

Word of Skipper's heroism reached Great Paradise and the community was immensely proud of its magnificent canine hero and treated him like royalty. However, Skipper had lost his former exuberance and spent much of his time resting as though exhausted by his trials. Sadly, a month later, and despite the efforts of Captain Ryan, Skipper died one night without a whimper.

Ryan knew that the effort expended by Skipper in saving his master was the cause of his death. According to a veterinarian the strain of waging that heroic battle for more than six hours had exhausted Skipper's great strength and had overtaxed his heart.

Captain Ryan and his family placed Skipper in a coffin and buried him in Great Paradise beside a large stone upon which they painted the inscription, "Here lies the remains of a truly great hero, a Newfoundland Dog named Skipper."

Newfoundland fishermen and Newfoundland dogs have shared many adventures, not the least of which is the case of a dog substituting for a captain. This following story is recounted by Booth Chern in *The New Complete Newfoundland*. Captain James Dibbon skippered his schooner *Jack Frost* out of Burin on the South Coast of Newfoundland in the 1930s. Having sailed the area for years he knew every sunker* and shoal along that shore. If it was foggy or stormy he relied on his dry compass, an old brass watch, and his dog, Laddie. The dog's father had also sailed with the seventy-year-old Dibbon, but had been swept overboard and lost in a storm.

Grey-muzzled Laddie had sailed on *Jack Frost* with Dibbon for more than ten years, but the old dog still had a deafening bark and was the best lookout on the coast. He warned his master of shoals or of surf breaking over rocks long before anyone else could, and every vessel along the south shore knew his voice.

When heading for Burin, Dibbon usually set his run straight for a sunker* that he knew of and, in the dead of night or in thick fog, Dibbon and Laddie stood at the bow listening for the breakers they knew were out there somewhere. When they neared the rock, Laddie's bark alerted his captain so he could give the concerned helmsman the order to put about and reach for Burin.

One Christmas Eve Dibbon left St. John's for home in the midst of a furious blizzard. A southwest wind was bringing a following sea and as the schooner rounded Cape Race, the double-reefed foresail gybed.* The boom struck Dibbon, flattening him, but luckily he wasn't swept overboard, having become entangled in a line.

Dibbon was taken unconscious to the cabin and the mate, though he was very young, had to take over. Running before the gale, he couldn't put about and return to St. John's with losing every spar, and so he had to continue. In the bow Laddie remained on watch, sheathed in ice and snow, dutifully sniffing to leeward and checking for the breakers. The mate had no choice but to rely on him; he'd made it home before with Dibbon beside him, and he could do it again with Laddie's help. The venerable dog duly warned him of the sunker and they maintained the proper course. Laddie appeared to study the sea and sky, occasionally grumbling with concern, and the boy followed the dog's guidance. Early Christmas morning the *Jack Frost*, its rigging encased in ice, sailed into the harbour at Burin.

Around 1935, Captain Walter Carter of Greenspond, Newfoundland, uncle of the former Member of Parliament of the same name, was fishing off Cape Mugford, north of Nutak, Labrador. The seventy-five-ton *Maggie Stone* was anchored in Mugford Tickle* while he and two of his crew jigged* from a skiff. Carter's Newfoundland stood in the stern of the schooner watching the small boat, which disappeared from view at times, as swells intervened.

Unexpectedly, a terrific squall struck, overturning the skiff. All three fishers were dumped into the frigid water and Carter, unable to swim, grabbed a gunwale and held on. In the rough water he had no idea where the other two were.

He hung on obstinately, but was rapidly losing his grip on the boat in the paralysing water, when suddenly he saw his dog coming directly toward him. The dog had seen the skiff capsize and had gone to the rescue before other members of the crew were even aware of the accident. In his cold-induced torpor and confusion Carter didn't understand that the dog had come all the way from the schooner; he assumed that he wanted something to climb onto in an effort to save himself. The terrified Carter's chilled hands lost their hold on the boat and he sank, remaining underwater and out of the dog's grasp as long as he could, then he rose to look around.

His schooner was barely visible through the spume and wind-whipped water, but he was thankful he had escaped the dog. He once more grasped the gunwale and hoped he could hold on until help came.

You can imagine the effect on Carter when he again saw the big dog materialize out of the spindrift and heard his heavy breathing as he bore down on him. For sheer terror there's probably nothing equal to being in the freezing North Atlantic, unable to swim, and having a 160 pound animal seemingly trying to use you as a flotation device.

Mustering his remaining energy, Carter let go and sank again. He opened his eyes underwater and looked up to see the big dog circling and circling. Panic-stricken, he prayed, but this time he lost consciousness.

He came to his senses to find that his dog had an unshakable grip on his jacket and was thrusting his half-frozen body through the waves. He lapsed into unconsciousness again and when he recovered he was on the deck of his schooner, the crew priming him with rum and his anxious dog licking his hands. The men hadn't had time to launch a dory and the two who had been in the skiff with Carter were never found.

When Captain Mike Augot's 140-ton schooner *Pauline E. Lohnes* was run down by the 3500-ton Belgian steamer *Jean Jadot* on June 17, 1937, the Newfoundland Monge was on board. The six dories that were out fishing took the remaining crew off the stricken vessel and all twenty-three men were taken on board the steamer, Monge being the last to leave the schooner. He and the crew were finally landed at the India Wharf at the foot of North Pier Street in Brooklyn, New York, and were lodged at the Seamen's Institute.

The *New York Times* reported (and Booth Chern quotes,in *The New Complete Newfoundland)* that Augot bemoaned the loss of his ship, charts, sextant and all his personal belongings. "With no ship and no cod-fishing supplies," he said, "the crew will be destitute." However, he found solace in not having lost Monge. "I wouldn't take $50 for him"—the equivalent of about $5000 today. "He's the best dog in the world," he told the reporter. Eight-year-old Monge had spent seven years sailing with the Newfoundland fishing fleet and Augot had taught him to retrieve seabirds. "As soon as Monge caught sight of the bird I shot, he dove overboard, swam to the bird, grasped it in his mouth and swam back to the ship, where he was hauled aboard," Augot explained.

No one had the heart to separate Monge from his captain. Rules were broken and the dog was allowed in the Institute bedroom with Augot. The next day both dog and master travelled by bus to Boston and there boarded a ship for Newfoundland.

The Newfoundland may not be completely amphibious, but the dogs don't seem to know that. Conrad Clarke of North Sydney, Nova Scotia, tells of an occasion in the mid-1990s when he and his wife had a small sailboat. Their dog loved to sail, and sometimes decided to ride in the small rowboat that they usually towed. One day they were steaming along at eight knots, or about ten miles an hour, when Clarke felt a drag on the sailboat. When his wife, Elizabeth, looked back, only the stern of the towed boat was out of the water, and no dog was in sight. Clarke quickly brought the larger vessel to a halt and the towed boat slowly re-emerged, dog and all. The boat had been entirely underwater and the dog, unfazed, had remained sitting in it.

Chapter 10

Nanny and Caregiver Extraordinaire

Big black puppy dog
name of Tug
lies by my bed
like a black bear rug.
> —Rose Burgunder in Smith, *Newfoundland Holiday*

This first verse of a poem by Rose Burgunder sums up the dog's association with children. Its great size and gentleness make it a capable and safe companion for everyone, and for generations it has been the traditional playmate and protector of his owners' children. Not easily hurt by small tugging fingers as a smaller dog might be, the Newfoundland undertakes the duties of a nanny of its own accord and without training. As a guardian of children its admirers give it many points, some even implying it is the solution to all babysitting problems.

A German print from the late 1800s, probably an advertisement, perfectly captures the relationship between a Newfoundland and a child.

Many others have noted this as well. In an old children's alphabet picture book, the letter *N* has a picture of a Newfoundland and the text reads:

> *N* is for Newfoundland—loyal and kind,
> better protector you never could find
> —from the Father Tuck series' *Cock-a-Doodle Do!*

Another verse, by an unknown writer from the late 1800s, also bears witness to the dog's popularity and reputation:

> I am the noble Newfoundland,
> My voice is loud and deep;
> I keep a watch all through the night
> While other people sleep.
> —from Drury, *This is the Newfoundland*

The dogs seem to gravitate toward children. Margaret Booth Chern reports in *The New Complete Newfoundland* that years ago a school teacher had a dog, another Neptune, who visited the playground regularly to romp with the young students. His favourite toy was the hoop, which he chased, caught, and grasped so that it rose above him and encircled his head. Then he paraded around, defying all and sundry to take it from him.

To him, snowball fights were wonderful. He would stand resolute but friendly while practically everyone in the schoolyard threw snowballs at him. Never short tempered, he barked and tried to catch the snowballs, leaping about and making mock charges at the children, all of them his friends.

In the same book, Booth Chern tells the tale of a rescue that proves there are threats to children other than deep water. In Kentucky's Fork Mountain area, in the 1800s, eagles often attempted to pick off a lamb or snatch up a chicken now and then.

In 1896, one seems to have very nearly made off with, or at least injured, a child! We've all heard such tales, usually with belief suspended, as an eagle cannot possibly lift more than four or five pounds. This particular eagle hadn't heard that. Two-year-old Willie Slone was playing outside with the family's Newfoundland when the possibly near-sighted eagle pounced on the youngster and sank its talons into his side. The dog grabbed the threshing bird by the leg and dragged it from its intended lunch, then held on until the boy's father came and killed it. It had a wingspread of more than seven feet.

In one terrible instance fate stepped in and kept a good Samaritan from doing her duty. The Barrows family lived in Rahway, New Jersey, their property bordering the fast-running Rahway River. In 1889 they had a Newfoundland dog, Dinah, the constant companion and playmate of their ten-year-old daughter, Annie. Dinah considered that her most important responsibility was to keep the girl away from the river.

When a greengrocer came to the front gate Annie's mother, in a bid to keep Dinah away from the man, chained her to her kennel and went to buy vegetables. As she neared the gate, she heard the dog's frenzied howling and for a moment wondered what the problem could be. Suddenly it dawned on her that something must be wrong; racing to the backyard she was in time to see Annie disappear beneath the churning waters while Dinah struggled, slowly dragging her kennel toward the river.

In another case, a small boy of New Rochelle, New York, took his dog when he went skating on Long Island Sound, a body of water that seldom freezes solid. Little George Foster had not been skating very long when he broke through the ice, and was struggling just to keep a grip on the edge of the ice. His Newfoundland recognized the difficulty and, not wanting to end up in the water as well, he crept on his belly until he got close enough to grab the boy's coat. Unable to pull George out, he nevertheless managed to keep his head above water until men from the nearby New Rochelle Yacht Club reached them and finished the rescue.

This story of a Newfoundland that sacrificed his life for his small charge appeared in the *Topeka State Journal* around the end of the nineteenth century:

> Sam Dodge, a ranchman living southeast of Caney, went to Vinita, Indian Territory, on business and shortly after he had gone, Bessie, his five-year-old child, wandered away from home in an attempt to follow him. Mrs. Dodge discovered her absence about two hours after Sam's departure. She made a thorough search of the premises, and failing to find the child, notified the neighbors of her disappearance. They turned out in force, and scoured the prairies all that day and all that night and all the next day, searching for the little wanderer.
>
> Late Saturday evening, an Indian came upon her fast asleep, just south of Post Oak Creek, in an old road known as the "Whiskey Trail." Across her body stood a Newfoundland

dog, which had always been her companion about the ranch. The dog was torn and bleeding, and near his feet lay the bodies of two wolves. Although her cheeks were stained with tears and covered with dust, Bessie was unharmed. She and her protector were taken back to her home, a distance of twelve miles from where they were found, where the dog died of his wounds that night. He was given a decent burial, and yesterday Sam Dodge ordered a marble monument, which will be placed at the head of the faithful animal's grave.

—quoted in Booth Chern, *The New Complete Newfoundland*

The tale of Pup, who lived from 1902 until 1916, was passed on by an H. E. Reimer of Sydney, Australia. Pup loved playing hide-and-seek, and he was equally adept at many other games. He also fetched the paper and carried things, but was not particularly trained for any chores.

When Reimer was six years old, he attended a school some five hundred yards from his house. One day, when he set out for school, the weather was sunny and warm. As the day wore on rain clouds blew in and his mother began worrying that he, having just gotten over a cold, would get his feet wet. Not quite seriously she told Pup to take the boy's rubber boots to him. She was astounded when the dog picked up the boots, walked out the door, and headed for the school; he returned in a short time without them.

The boy was just as surprised when his dog walked into the school with the boots, picked his way between the desks to his young master, and dropped them on the floor. He poked the boy with his nose and left. Pup had never been to the school before and never went back.

Notwithstanding the folly or obstinacy of their clients, Newfoundland dogs never seem to get discouraged and say "Oh, forget it!" On Saturday, June 13, 1936, the overseas edition of the London *Daily Mail* carried a photograph of little Roland Sprowson, who had a fine instinct for self destruction, with a Newfoundland dog, Rex. It accompanied the following story:

> ...[Rex] has just been awarded the bronze medal of the Canine Defence League for saving [Roland's] life a third time. Roland had wandered from home to the banks of the Humber. "Rex" was seen to edge him away from the water, and when the boy toddled towards the railway lines along which an express train was due, "Rex" pulled him back.
> —quoted in MacPherson, *The Book of Newfoundland*

In the mid-1950s Margaret Booth Chern received a letter from Mary Lyons telling her about eleven-year-old Tarby, who had taken the duty of babysitter upon himself and was very serious about it. In it she said that if she was busy and the child began to cry she simply told Tarby to go up and check on the baby. Going upstairs he would enter the baby's room, nudge him a little, then lie down beside the crib until Lyons arrived. Further, she said the boy idolized Tarby and when he was learning to walk he often fell on the dog and climbed all over him.

In a *Dog Fancy* magazine article from August 1994, Megan Nutbeem recalls five lives saved by dogs from her Harbourbeem Kennels. One was a ten-year-old boy, whose dog hated the water but saved him from drowning.

Another was a small child whose dog saved also her from drowning, this time in the family pool. When the child's mother went looking for her after not seeing her for a while, she found the little girl in the pool, hanging onto the back of their diligent and exhausted Newfoundland. The dog had been paddling around the pool for who knows how long, unable to climb out because there were no steps. In fact, the spent dog needed help getting out.

The Newfoundland's instinct for rescuing children was vividly illustrated in 1983, and reported by Emily D'Aulaire and Per Ola in a *Reader's Digest* article called "The Bravest Dog."

The blizzard of 1983 struck Villas, New Jersey, near Cape May on the east side of Delaware Bay, on February 11. That afternoon Lynda and Dick Veit took their three Newfoundlands for a walk on the beach in front of their house. The wind was so violent that just getting the front door open was a struggle. Upon returning home, one-year-old Villa (Dirigo's Magnificent Villa) wanted to go out again. While the other dogs napped, Dick Veit let her out and noted how much snow had fallen.

Next door, eleven-year-old Andrea Anderson and her two sisters had the day off school because of the storm. As they played in the snow, they could see the dark smudge that was Villa, in her run. Fourteen-year-old Diane and nine-year-old Heather soon decided it was too cold and went inside, but Andrea went to look at the bay and the storm-lashed waves.

Once she was away from the shelter of the house, a powerful blast of wind blew her forty or fifty feet and down a five-foot (one-and-a-half-metre) bank, where she landed in a deep snowdrift on the sand dunes. The water was only a few feet away.

Luckily for Andrea, Newfoundlands are able to withstand harsh temperatures when necessary.

She was unable to move in the tightly packed snow, and in any case, had no idea of the direction in which she should move. She was shocked by the blinding mixture of sand and snow. Crying out in fright, though no one could hear her, she desperately tried to climb free. She was hoarse from shouting and her hands and feet were numb; her face, half-frozen and raw from the wind, snow, and sand, ached terribly.

From her pen, Villa heard Andrea's faint cries despite the wind. She leapt over the five-foot fence and dashed to the beach. When the big dog materialized through the drifting snow Andrea didn't realize her rescuer had arrived, but she was happy to see her anyway.

Villa bounded through the snow to lick Andrea's freezing face, then tramped round and round packing the snow down. When she was satisfied she stopped and, bracing herself, thrust her great head toward the girl. Andrea's arms encircled Villa's neck and the dog struggled backward, pulling Andrea free of the snowdrift to a space blown relatively free of snow.

Staggering to her feet, Andrea fixed both hands in Villa's fur, then stumbled along the beach and up a small sheltered ravine, Villa breaking trail for her. On top of the bank the full driving force of the wind struck, knocking Andrea to the ground again and again.

Whenever she fell, Villa went back and patiently waited for her to regain her grip, then plodded on. In this manner it took fifteen minutes to cover the short distance back to the house.

Bea Anderson, Andrea's mother, saw the shapes pass the window and realized she hadn't seen any of the girls since she heard them come in forty-five minutes earlier. She opened the door and saw Andrea, cold and ashen, who blurted, "Mom, Villa just saved my life." Her astonished mother listened as a tearful Andrea told her tale.

Villa went home, scratched on the front door and was let in, covered with snow. At the same time Bea Anderson telephoned with the story and the heroine was treated to a steak dinner.

New Jersey's Senator Bill Bradley took the floor of the United States Senate and read a document into the Congressional Record lauding Villa for her "outstanding loyalty and intelligence," and as the "bravest dog in America." She was honoured by the Newfoundland Club of America as the "Heroic Newfoundland of 1983," and was also selected as Ken-L Ration Dog Hero of the Year.

A limousine took Villa, the Andersons, and the Veits to Washington where, on February 29, 1984, she attended a special ceremony at the vice-presidential mansion. First Lady Barbara Bush hung a gold medal on a red, white, and blue ribbon around Villa's neck.

Nutbeem also observed that the dogs seemed to have a wonderful understanding of when to guard and when not. Nutbeem's first child, Robin, spent quite a lot of time outside in a perambulator, and there was always a Newfoundland dog beside the carriage. Visitors could talk to the baby, but were not permitted to get between the dog and the pram. One fall day a solicitous aunt thought it was too cold for the child to be outdoors and, unsuspecting, attempted to take her inside. Hearing a commotion, Nutbeem came to the door to find her aunt sitting astride the dog, backward, with arms and legs flailing, being rapidly transported across the yard. The look of amazement on the aunt's face was apparently indescribable. The dog deposited her gently on the ground by sitting down and letting her slide off, then returned to lie down, unruffled, by the baby's carriage.

Another babysitting story from the Nutbeems concerns the disciplining of their children so as not to produce "spoiled brats." They rejected the efforts of grandparents to rock the baby when she cried, and their methods worked well—they had a well-behaved and happy baby who seldom cried.

They were perhaps too proud of this fact; when friends came by for morning coffee the Nutbeems told them of their exceptional training methods. Megan Nutbeem was mortified when, nearly a full year later, she glanced out a neighbour's window to see her dog Jill giving the baby carriage a gentle push. It would rock for some time, slow, come to a stop, then get another nudge. She called her friends, who had, it turned out, been watching the babysitter since the child had been first put outdoors—to their great amusement, considering the Nutbeems' boastfulness.

Clayton was the first assistance dog of Kathy Catliss of Grand Rapids, Michigan. Interviewed on the CBC's *Land and Sea* on February 13, 2001, and March 26, 2004, she called him her "guardian angel."

In 1994, Kathy began to lose the use of her arms, legs, and shoulders, because of a rare muscular disorder that left her confined to a wheelchair. Her search for a dog led her to a breeder of Newfoundlands, and while she visited the breeder, she dropped her pen. One of four puppies who were sleeping at her feet picked it up and held it until she could retrieve it. She quickly made her decision.

Clayton, who outweighed his diminutive owner by forty-odd pounds, opened doors for her, both physically and emotionally. He was at her side during all her medical tests and, with amazing patience, would pick up a dropped item and place it in her hand twenty times if necessary.

Pal was a good friend to Jack Hayden, Mike Ratcliffe and Eileen Chafe—their stories can be found in the "Warrior" chapter.

He pulled her wheelchair as well as a small cart she used when shopping and was always eager to learn. At four months of age he demonstrated his ability to sense when she was about to have a seizure and would give warning. To provide the necessary "hit" that would raise her blood sugar level, he would bring her a Coke from the refrigerator and place it in her hand. As bad as a nagging parent, he would stand watching as she drank and showed his disgust if she hesitated or didn't finish.

Kathy taught Clayton to press the telephone speed-dial with his paw to call 911, then explained to her local emergency telephone operators that if a dog was heard barking from her phone number they were to come to her home. Three times she has regained consciousness to find paramedics in attendance. Clayton had used his own judgement and called them. He began to slow down in 2001 and was diagnosed as having severe arthritis, so Kathy found another Newfoundland that same year to take his place. Clayton remained on the job and helped train the new dog, Garrett, but, unhappily, had to be euthanised in 2002. Kathy has stipulated that each of her assistance dogs be cremated and their ashes buried with hers after her death.

Dogs can be therapeutic for those suffering from autism, depression, or other mental disorders; indeed, most anyone, particularly the infirm, can benefit from the ministrations of a therapy dog. It's surprising how well patients respond to the advances of a friendly Newfoundland.

Mary Lou Naso's sons told the My Hero website about Naso and her Newfoundland, who visit the sick and dying. Well-behaved Harry pays loving attention to the people he visits and performs tricks for their entertainment if appropriate. Every two weeks they visit the Children's Center for Rehabilitation and the Rainbow Babies and Children's Hospital, both in Cleveland, Ohio.

Harry's visits usually include treats and petting. Some of the more able-bodied children play ball with him, and he likes to catch and retrieve. He also performs tricks, knows his left paw from his right, and can guess the hand in which you are hiding a treat, indicating the hand by placing a large paw on it. He has free rein at the hospital and is allowed in all the units, even intensive care.

Naso and Harry attended special obedience classes for eight months preparing him to become a licensed "Therapy Dog." Afterward, he was tested by Therapy Dog International to ensure he was ready for the unusual situations that can be encountered by the dog and owner in a hospital. Given obedience-testing commands while interacting with those in wheelchairs and on crutches, Harry passed with flying colours. A bedpan was even dropped behind him in a bid to startle him but he showed not a flicker of concern and was among the top dogs in his class.

Naso and Harry bring smiles to people who may not smile very much. One mother came out of a hospital room and asked if her son could meet the dog, but when the two entered they found the boy comatose after brain surgery to remove a tumour. The mother placed her son's hand on Harry's head and explained to the unconscious boy that he was stroking a black dog, like a Labrador, and helped him rub the dog's fur. She smiled and thanked them before they left, saying that she knew her son would remember Harry.

Naso and Harry are well-nigh idolized for the happiness they spread throughout the hospital.

It's not surprising that the Newfoundland could be such an excellent therapy dog; they are very well known for being in tune with the feelings of others. In January 2004, schoolgirl Cassandra Fortier of Kars, Ontario, had been having a difficult day. Nothing major, just a series of annoyances, but when she slipped and fell while coming downstairs it was the last straw and she burst into tears. Her mother, Amber, went to her, put an arm around her shoulders and consoled her while they both sat on a step.

When Bear (Rebecca's Water Bear) came to see what the fuss was about, Amber realized that he had something in his mouth. Normally, he pulled away if someone attempted to take something from him, but this time he edged closer and closer to Cassandra as Amber tried to see what he had. She found that he had taken fresh facial tissues from the pocket of her sweater and brought them to the unhappy pair. Unfortunately the absorbent paper had gotten soggy and stuck in his mouth.

Chapter 11

Protector

Intelligent and with the strength and temperament to carry out all the exploits ascribed to him, the Newfoundland is an effective guard and watchdog.

Hearing a basso-profondo bark and seeing a dog with his paws on top of a four-foot fence and towering one or two feet above it would cause any would-be burglar to pause and reflect on their career choice. The dog, as we have learned, seems to have an inbred ability to differentiate between friend and foe, and if well-meaning visitors steel themselves to approach this formidable-looking guard, they will find a tail wagging and gentle greeting. Visitors with less noble intentions may find a rather more ferocious dog, and any other animal threatening a Newfoundland's loved ones is immediately dealt with.

In *The Sportsman's Repository*, Sir Robert Scott described a friend's dog, Jowler*:

> The dog Jowler, after many hard-fought battles, and when he had attained his full growth, soon established his character for superiority. He was not quarrelsome, but treated the smaller species of dogs with patience and forbearance; but when attacked by a dog of equal size, or engaged in restoring peace among other dogs, he would set to, most vigorously, and continue the struggle until submission was obtained, or peace completely re-established. He would then leave the

field of battle with a haughty look, and a warning growl, and be afterwards as quiet as a lamb. His master was perfectly secure in his company; for the least appearance of an attack on his person, raised at once the dog's attention, and produced a most tremendous growl as the signal of action, in his master's defence. The sagacity of this animal is astonishing, and on all occasions he seemed to want only the faculty of speech to place his intellect on a level with the human.

One tale of a devoted protector was told by an old man to newspaperman P. W. Latham of New York in the late 1800s, and recorded by Booth Chern in *The New Complete Newfoundland*. Neptune had been taken from a brutal owner and attached himself to his rescuer's young son. When illness beset the child, Neptune remained at his side and from then on refused to be separated from him. He saved him from drowning when the boy was six or seven, and from an even more terrifying predicament a decade later, when the boy was in his late teens. The boy left some friends while on a walk in the forest, and found a strange and engaging kitten. As he bent to pick the animal up, a terrific scream rent the air and a great weight struck his back. The teeth and claws of a large panther tore at him and he fell heavily to the ground, striking his head and passing out.

After some time his friends found and revived him. Neptune was missing and the turf, leaves, and brush had been disturbed all around the area. The boy and his friends searched until they found the faithful old dog; in the heated battle he had waged with the boy's attacker, both fell down an appallingly steep cliff and both had died.

A Newfoundland from the time of Scott's writings in the *Sportsman's Repository*.

It doesn't seem to matter how large or how threatening the danger may be, the Newfoundland is willing to tackle it, as is pointed out in this story from Patrick Pickett's *Heroic Companion*. Around 1920 not many people in Newfoundland, let alone dogs, were familiar with railroads. Harold MacPherson's Oscar was eight years old when his family went to watch a train roar by. The dog accompanied them, standing just off the rails. The snorting locomotive startled Oscar as it suddenly rounded a nearby curve and he, unwisely, attempted to save his master from the horror bearing down on them by throwing himself at the thing. He suffered severe head injuries, and though he survived, he could no longer tell friend from foe (one may argue that he had to have trouble in this area to come by his injuries) and had to be muzzled when strangers were present.

Boatswain (Little Bear's Boatswain)—yes, another Boatswain—was probably the closest friend noted jazz pianist Carlos Cortez had. It made little difference where or at what hour of the night Cortez played at a nightclub, Boatswain waited patiently in the car. Once in the 1940s, after entertaining at a club in Detroit, Cortez headed for his car at 4:00 a.m., having to walk four or five blocks. About halfway there he was jumped by a gang of knife-wielding teenagers.

Luckily, Cortez drove a convertible: Boatswain, hearing the struggle, tore through the canvas top and raced to help. He landed among Cortez's assailants like a whirlwind; unwilling to face an animal of such size and ferocious disposition, they ran. Cortez suffered only minor cuts and bruises and allowed that, though he was a strong man, he could not have held off his armed attackers very long and was nearly played out when his friend showed up.

One Christmas another of Harold MacPherson's Westerland dogs, Sieger (Ch. Westerland Sieger), went to the assistance of a stranger. A nurse on her way home was accosted by a drunk who insisted on walking with her. Sieger, in his yard, noticed them and somehow detected a disagreement between the two. He rushed out to the sidewalk with a deep growl that startled and discouraged the would-be swain, who quickly left. Sieger, tail waving slowly, escorted the nurse to her door then strolled back home.

Incidentally, this was the same dog that, in 1937, shared with King George VI the two postage stamps issued by Newfoundland and the Commonwealth to honour the latter's coronation.

One family taking a summer vacation at a cottage in the woods of Nova Scotia was accompanied by their Newfoundland dog. On an exceptionally fine day, the man and his dog went for a stroll and encountered an ill-mannered and grouchy bear.

The bear charged the man but was surprised by the 170-pound dog that flung himself into his path and forced him back. The bear made numerous attempts to reach the man, but the dog persevered and held him back, avoiding the attacks for the most part. The bear eventually gave up and left, and the man took his injured friend to a veterinarian. His wounds were unexpectedly light and he recovered quickly.

A *Downhome* article from 2000 shows that at least one other Newfoundland has taken on a bear and won. Conrad and Elizabeth Clarke of North Sydney, Nova Scotia, took their family and seven-year-old dog Sam to their summer home at Jersey Cove, Cape Breton Island, in September 1999. Elizabeth was feeding small animals in the nearby woods one day, suspecting nothing. Evidently a prowling bear approached a little too closely to Sam's family and he picked up the scent.

The dogs often have magnificent guarding skills, as exhibited here by Boatswain.

Conrad recounted, "We heard a loud crashing sound in the woods. Now we guess that must have been Sam going after the bear."

Exactly what happened between the dog and bear no one will ever know, but at the house that evening Sam didn't appear to be injured. The next morning, however, a terrible smell was coming from the dog. Elizabeth and her daughter Roschell, both nurses, knew immediately that the odour indicated a serious infection. Sam was taken to a veterinarian at once and beneath the dog's dense coat the problem was found: bites and claw marks, evidence of a desperate fight with a bear. Holes left by the bear's teeth were an inch deep, and the vet remarked that the bear probably suffered a cracked tooth during the scrap. Sam had bruises from the bear's club-like paws, and deep claw marks as well. The Clarkes realized their dog had received his wounds protecting the family from a danger none of them had even been aware of. The 186-pound dog had clearly held his own quite well.

Sam recovered from the attack but tragically, almost exactly a year later, he ate some grass contaminated with a pesticide. He died at the age of seven on September 11, 2000, and was buried at Jersey Cove.

Around 1970, Booth Chern reports in *The New Complete Newfoundland*, Panda and her owner Paul Katzoff were driving from New York City to their home in Aspen, Colorado, in late summer. Most of the time, one-year-old Panda was apparently occupied with the sights of this new adventure. On a sizzling night, while crossing Kansas, Katzoff began to feel drowsy and sensibly pulled off the road for a nap.

Because of the heat he wound the windows down and was shockingly awakened when someone suddenly pulled him from the car and threw him to the ground. A fist thudded into his face and he knew—this was it. Stunned and hurt, he was about to be murdered by three or four thugs.

As the world dissolved about him he suddenly became aware of Panda. Someone was shrieking in panic and he realized his young dog had clamped her powerful jaws on his assailant's thigh. Panda dragged the assailant off Katzoff and rushed at a second man, smashing him down. The surprised and terrified attackers turned tail and ran.

Dean and Grace Edwards of Coquitlam, British Columbia, owned a six-year-old Newfoundland, J. J., and they thought he might like to have a friend. Having known Newfoundland breeders Judi and

Ellis Adler of Portland, Oregon (who tell this story on their website, www.sweetbay.com), for years, they were admirers of their Sweetbay dogs and asked them for a Landseer puppy.

The Adlers had only one and said they had no intention of selling her. But persistence paid off, and the Edwardses became the new owners of seven-month-old Lindsey (Sweetbay's Lindsey) on Mothers' Day, 1990.

Lindsey soon learned not to bark and disturb the neighbours and things went smoothly. But a month after she joined the family, on Fathers' Day, she roused the family with frenzied barking at 2:00 a.m. Dean yelled at her to stop, but when Lindsey paid no attention he became concerned; something had to be amiss.

Dean thought he heard shouting between Lindsay's barks and listened more intently. The people next door had separated, and divorce was pending. The volatile husband had apparently ignored a restraining order and, knowing the man's record of previous assaults, Dean told Grace to call the police.

When someone pounded on their door Dean opened it to find their neighbour, Joanne, bleeding and badly injured. Moments later the police arrived and found Joanne's husband rushing about in a frenzy with a bloodied hammer, looking for her, and he was taken into custody.

The police told the Edwardses that the man had furiously demanded some time with their children on Father's Day, but in accordance with the court order Joanne had refused. He had waited until early morning then crept onto the property and tried the doors. Finding them locked, he threw a large stone though the glass and entered.

Joanne awakened to find him looming over her, screaming and swinging a hammer. He struck her on the head and when she tried

to shield her face he broke her arm. Seriously injured, she attempted to crawl away and he swung again, severing tendons in her foot.
A house guest, awakened by Lindsey's furious barking next door,
interrupted the attack and allowed a few moments for Joanne to
escape.

Lindsey had put up a fuss as soon as the husband had set foot
on the property. After a month of being taught not to bark she had
learned well, yet she had barked when it mattered. Had she not
sounded the alarm, the guest would not have interrupted the attack
and the police would not have been called in time.

Police gave the dog full credit for the rescue and there was
no doubt that the husband had murder in mind. For several
weeks after the incident Lindsey patrolled her yard with extra
vigilance.

When a Newfoundland barks or growls there's usually a valid reason. Mauzy's owner, Amber Fortier, wrote in a personal letter that
she had heard Mauzy growl only once:

> I think it was one of the nastiest sounds I've ever heard; all
> the more so because it was so unfamiliar. We were staying in
> a cabin while on vacation in Newfoundland and had gotten
> a reduced rate because the cabin we had checked into was
> undergoing repairs and was not quite ready.
>
> Mauzy heard someone outside and emitted a sound unlike
> anything I'd heard from her before or since; scared the pants
> off me.
>
> A man had come to continue work on the exterior of the
> cabin and hadn't been aware it had been rented the night

before. When we went outside, he was sitting on a sawhorse a fair distance away, looking a little pale.

So, if your Newfoundland has something say—listen, and look around.

Chapter 12

Warrior

Certainly not a belligerent creature by nature, the Newfoundland nevertheless sees it as his duty to help his silly, quarrelling friends. He's been present on many fields of battle and on many a man-of-war and has always given a good account of himself.

As seagoing dogs, Newfoundlands were popular mascots on many warring ships. Booth Chern, in *The New Complete Newfoundland,* tells the story of Victor. During the Napoleonic Wars (1792–1815), Victor was with the seventy-four-gun HMS *Bellona,* a third-rater of about 1200 tons with a crew of more than five hundred men. At the Battle of Copenhagen, which began on April 2, 1801, he fearlessly remained on deck for hours, through the thick of the fight. *Bellona* was eventually put out of the battle when it and HMS *Russell* ran aground. Victor, because of his valiant efforts and continued presence during the action, was very highly thought of by the crew, who spread the word of their exceptional fighting dog throughout the fleet.

When *Bellona* was paid off following the Peace of Amiens in 1802, the sailors held a parting dinner ashore and Victor had the place of honour. He was seated at the table and given the same roast beef and figgy-dowdy* as his comrades. In fact, the dinner menu was dedicated to the hero and bore his name.

During the same conflict, Grant Young reports in *Downhome,* the frigate HMS *Nymph* joined in combat with the French *Cleopatra.* On board *Nymph* was a stalwart Newfoundland who had never before seen naval action. Despite the confusion, noise, smoke, and fire, and although the crew tried to keep him below, he resisted their endeavours and remained on deck throughout the engagement. Undaunted by the thunderous firing of the frigate's forty guns, he "barked and exhibited violent rage throughout the battle." After some hours of exchanging heavy fire, the ships closed and fought yardarm to yardarm until *Cleopatra* finally struck its colours. When the English boarding party went over the Frenchman's side, the dog was the first onto its bloody deck. He proudly stalked from stem to stern, observing the actions of his friends and keeping a keen eye on his recent enemies, who cringed at his approach.

In 1861, during the American Civil War, the 10th Maine Regiment were preparing to move south by rail when a large Newfoundland appeared in Company H's railway coach. He seemed to believe he belonged there and his friendly attitude and imposing aspect greatly impressed the soldiers. Having no idea who he belonged to or where he had come from, they adopted him as their mascot and named him Major. His adventures are recorded by Kenneth L. Roberts in *Trending into Maine*.

Major was selective in his choice of friends and didn't usually mix with men of other companies. The one notable exception occurred after his capture by Confederate soldiers during the retreat from Winchester, Virginia, on May 25, 1862. He condescended to recognize another prisoner, a soldier from his regiment's Company F. Eventually, he and his new friend escaped together and Major rejoined his comrades soon after they reached Union lines.

At the battle of Cedar Mountain, Virginia, on August 9, Major accompanied the leading troops into the fray and came through unscathed. The following month, at the battle of Antietam in Maryland, he again fought ferociously beside his friends.

The 10th Maine Regiment was mustered out in May of 1863, and Major followed many of his old comrades in the 29th Maine and continued his actions against the enemy for a year. At the battle of Mansfield, in Louisiana, on April 8, 1864, Major fought courageously until he was killed on the field of battle by a Confederate Minié ball. His loss was greatly mourned by his comrades-in-arms.

In April 1917, during World War One, one of MacPherson's dogs, two-year-old Sable (Westerland's Sable Chief), was acquired through the efforts of Sir Edgar Bowring and presented to the Second Battalion of the Royal Newfoundland Regiment at Ayr, Scotland. Private Hazen M. Fraser was appointed dog-master.

Sable was big, with a majestic bearing. He attended all parades, marching ahead of the band, and when the national anthem was played he came to his feet of his own accord and stood at attention. Off duty he behaved like the big playful puppy he was and the soldiers held him in high esteem.

Sable earned the lasting respect of his comrades for his bearing, deeds, and protective friendship. He was so respected that when he died after being struck by a truck, the Regiment had him preserved for posterity. Sable still stands in the Newfoundland Naval and Military Museum in the Confederation Building at St. John's.

The U.S. army employed Newfoundlands in World War Two, particularly in Alaska's Aleutian Islands. A technical manual of the time describes the Newfoundland: "A massive, powerful dog. Water resistant coat equips him for cold and wet weather. An excellent pack dog, he possesses talent for rescuing people." Patrick Pickett gives details about these amazing pack dogs in *Heroic Companion*.

Most of these dogs received rigorous training during the winter at Fort Remic, Montana, or at Fort Robinson, Nebraska, and when they arrived in the Aleutian Islands they were much better prepared than their handlers.

Though the average winter temperature there is around freezing, storms bring high winds, fog, snow, sleet, and rain. The harsh environment had little effect on the dogs and many preferred to sleep outside their kennels. In addition to their usual diet, they

The beautiful Landseer Wallace at a ceremonial dinner attended by British royalty in London, England, on December 6, 1945.

were given a copious measure of lard to provide the fat necessary for heavy work in the cold. The only concession to their forbidding environment was the donning of rawhide boots to protect their feet from the jagged rock and ice.

Teams of four dogs carried their loads over the rugged terrain through deep snow and soaking rains, often in freezing temperatures. They also guided their soldiers safely through the storms. They could handle a surprising weight and delivered to outlying positions up to 1,200 pounds of dry clothing, ammunition, pigeon coops, spare parts, and rations.

Because the camps were far from the seashore, the dogs worke d uncomplainingly for as long as ten hours a day. At the end of these days of strenuous exertion, the exhausted soldiers said the dogs "acted as if they had been for a leisurely stroll in Central Park."

While highly thought of as pack animals, The Aleutian Islands dogs also laid telephone lines by carrying reels of wire on their backs that unrolled as they followed their masters to their destinations. It should also be mentioned that during the war some of them died in other theatres, in the hunt for land mines or while acting as couriers.

One war dog stands out above all others, regardless of breed. Pal, one of Harold MacPherson's Westerland puppies, was owned by American Rod Hayden, who was the Shell Oil agent at the Gander airfield when World War Two broke out. Pal was big even by Newfoundland standards, big enough to once cause an American pilot to report a bear on the runway.

Keeping Pal off the airstrip was only one of Hayden's problems. His dog loved children and in winter he willingly hauled the Hayden children and their friends around the base on a sled. Unluckily, one day the playful dog attempted to put his paws on the shoulders of a neighbour's child, Joan Chafe, and missed. A big claw scratched the little girl's face.

Joan's sister Eileen recalled that they all loved the dog, but worried about his actions around children. Hayden's wife offered Pal to a detachment of the 1st Battalion of the Royal Rifles of Canada stationed at Gander. Already a favourite of the young soldiers, Pal was accepted, turned into a regimental mascot, and renamed "Gander." Fred Kelly, his handler, fed him once a day and bathed him by putting him in the shower. Kelly said Gander was playful and affectionate, and enjoyed an occasional bowl of beer.

Gander was all but forgotten until around 1995, when Jeremy Swanson of the Canadian War Museum was working on a display for the Victoria Cross awarded to Sergeant Major John Osborn, who had flung himself on a grenade to save his companions. Swanson commented on the brave act to a veteran of a Hong Kong battle. The veteran replied, "Sure was. Just like that damned dog."

In 1997 the sister of the girl whom Pal/Gander had scratched many years before, now Eileen Elms, heard a short feature on CBC Radio One called, "That's a Good Question." This particular question was about whether a dog could be awarded a medal, as there was a Newfoundland dog named Gander who had reportedly saved soldiers' lives in Hong Kong.

The name roused Elm's interest and she wrote to the CBC. She was contacted and asked if she had a picture of Pal and she did; it was the same dog. A witness to the act of heroism was needed in order for him to be awarded a medal, and the search for a suitable witness began. Finally Lieutenant William B. Bradley, a native of

Sherbrooke, Quebec, who took part in the action with Gander, was interviewed at his home in Wilmette, Illinois, in 1999. He told of seeing the dog attacking Japanese soldiers, snarling and tearing at them. He didn't understand then or now why the Japanese didn't shoot him.

It transpired that in a move more political than military, Canada sent troops to help defend Hong Kong, including the Royal Rifles. Their mascot adapted well to military life.

By mid-December 1941, the Hong Kong garrison was engaged in a hopeless, last-ditch effort to hold off an overwhelming three divisions of the Japanese army. On Christmas Eve, Canadian soldiers were being killed in the streets of Hong Kong in their desperate bid to drive back the attackers. From the start, their battle had been a series of retreats, and after days of exhausting fighting they had their backs to the wall. Gander had already become a legend,

Sergeant Gander and an army buddy in 1941.

fighting alongside his friends and, on one occasion, forcing a squad of Japanese to change their course of attack on a small group of Canadians by charging at them.

The last stand began on Christmas Eve that night at eleven o'clock, in the face of a Japanese force that was, numerically, far superior to the tattered Canadian regiment. During the enemy's steady advance, hand grenades thrown at the Canadians were often scooped up and thrown back. Poor timing killed many playing this deadly game of catch.

Gander and his troop, many of them wounded, retired to a trench; then a hand grenade rolled in among them, its fuse smoking. No one but Gander could possibly reach it before it exploded; he scooped it up in his big mouth, leapt from the trench, and ran.

Bradley recalled that Gander was blown into pieces, and wondered whether he was just playing a game. But Gander had seen many grenades explode, and Bradley concluded that the noble dog was simply trying to take something dangerous away from his friends.

His action saved about twenty lives, and at long last, in August 2000, he was granted the Dickin Medal posthumously. For the first time since 1949 this animal-equivalent of the Victoria Cross, presented by the British organization People's Dispensary for Sick Animals, was awarded. Gander's old friend and handler, Fred Kelly, accepted it on his behalf.

Shamefully, the Canadian War Museum has not seen fit to erect a memorial to Sergeant Gander, though many support the idea. Perhaps some day we can erect one in his old hometown, whose name he bore with such honour.

Chapter 13

Trained Professionals

The Newfoundland's ability as a lifeguard and as a search-and-rescue agent is so exceptional that there are formal organizations devoted to training and employing the dogs. Breeders and owners of Newfoundlands believe the dogs must not only look good and have a fine temperament, but should be able to carry out their historic function—that of a water dog and rescuer. While the Newfoundland has an astonishing inherent ability in the water, it must be reinforced if our hero is to make a career of hauling folks out of that element. When so enhanced these rescue dogs are used worldwide.

This training has gone on for nearly two centuries now. In the early- to mid-1800s the city of Paris resolved to take advantage of the dogs' talent for rescue. Ten were selected and taken there to be used as rescue dogs along the Seine. After some training by the French police in rescuing dummies, both adult and child sized, the dogs went to work, and in a very short time proved invaluable. They later patrolled the beaches of the Bay of Biscay as well. During the summer of 1975 the dogs rescued dozens of swimmers who found themselves in trouble.

In the United States, Newfoundlands form the core of many search-and-rescue organizations, such as California's Black Paws. In Europe they've gained fame in other work: the Italian Army has a complete team of Newfoundland rescue dogs and handlers. Many

of these dogs have been trained to cross ravines on lifelines, para-
chute into inaccessible areas, rescue those trapped by avalanches,
and, naturally, help those in difficulty in the water.

In 1876 the British Kennel Association organized a series of water
trials for Newfoundlands, and drafted rules for their conduct. These
have prevailed virtually without modification. The dogs must: display courage by jumping into the water from a height to recover
a floating object; bring the object to shore quickly; display intelligence and speed in pulling a drifting boat to shore; carry a rope
from shore to a boat with a stranger (not the dog's master) in it;
show speed and power against a current or tide during a swimming
race; and dive for an object beneath the water. The Newfoundland
Club of America re-established water trials in 1956 and today these
and other tests, such as for obedience and carting, are sponsored
by various Newfoundland dog clubs. These are recognized by the
American Kennel Club, the Kennel Club (Britain), and the Canadian
Kennel Club. Rescue dogs must past these rigorous tests in order to
be officially certified.

Mas, the famous Newfoundland rescue dog, is a legend in Italy.
She earned the Italian title of First Canine Lifeguard when, around
1993, she rescued her owner's daughter Valentina and her friend,
who got in difficulty while swimming. The big black dog swam out
and, while Valentina clutched her fur and her friend held onto her
leash, Mas pulled both girls to shore.

Inspired by this, Valentina's father, Ferrucio Pilenga, with the
help of what proved to be an uncommon dog, set up the renowned
canine lifeguard school at Lago d'Iseo, northeast of Milan. The two
pioneered a new technique for saving lives—water rescue from a

helicopter. Mas leapt, apparently without fear, from a helicopter, swam to the would-be victims, and, with incredible strength, pulled them to safety.

At Pilenga's lifesaving school for aquatic canines, dogs train for more than a year. They spend much of that time learning not to do things as they are used to. The way they swim, for example, is corrected , allowing them to tow someone to shore without scratching them with their forefeet. If rescuing an unconscious swimmer, the dogs will grasp the upper arm and roll the person onto their backs, thus keeping the person's face out of the water. The most important things the dogs learn are that commands and signals must be obeyed unhesitatingly, and that they must endure the vagaries of the human mind. The training is possibly of even greater value to the handlers, who must learn more than the dogs.

Probably the most disconcerting thing the dogs must overcome are the conditions of helicopter operations. They must learn to dive and obey hand signals in the deafening rotor wash of the helicopter that turns the water to a slashing spray.

Although the veteran Mas is now nearly thirteen years old and suffering from arthritis, she is still a working dog helping to train new recruits so there will be many more canine lifeguards to follow in her pawprints. You will have perhaps seen the famed Mas leaping to the rescue in advertisements for the dog food Eukanuba.

In the late 1990s, Denise Castonguay of CastaNewf Kennels in Maple Ridge, British Columbia, saw vivid proof of Newfoundlands' lifesaving skills during a lakeside training session with Mister, a young Newfoundland bred at her kennel and sold to friends Christophe and Nicola Firstner. Castonguay worked on her dogs' water rescue skills at Buntzen Lake, a popular tourist destination where the water is clear and clean. This is one of the few lakes that both allows dogs and has a boat launch, essentials for water work-training.

One hot, cloudless morning, when sun-worshippers would be out in force, Casonguay and trainers arrived early with the dogs in an attempt to avoid the crowds, but by the time they'd finished their work the park was packed.

Preparing to leave, they had just loaded their boat onto its trailer when a group of teenagers arrived on the dock. The dogs, anxious to return to the water, had been tied up until they were ready to leave, and each teenaged whoop and splash into the water wound them up a little more. The boisterous teenagers were racing each other from the dock to a rocky point of land a few hundred yards away.

The dogs, following their instinctive drive, had no way of knowing the commotion was nothing more than kids having fun. Mister, in particular, could barely contain himself and although he now holds seventeen titles for his various skills, at the time he was just getting started. The temptation seemed to be more than his youthful enthusiasm could withstand and in a frenzy he broke free, charged straight for the end of the dock, and plunged into the water.

Castonguay tried everything she could think of to get Mister back to shore but he ignored her, circling near the end of the dock, whining. The teenagers were yelling and screaming louder than ever and she knew the only way to get her dog back was to take the boat out again and pick him up.

By then there were so many people at the dock that Castonguay suspected something else had happened. Even after being abruptly hauled out of the water, Mister remained intent on the crowd at the dock. By the time the boat was loaded again an ambulance had arrived, but it was much later in the day that they learned what had happened. One of the boys hadn't surfaced after leaping into the water, and divers had to be called in to retrieve his body.

Castonguay was astonished to learn that Mister had been circling over the same place where the body was found. He had known where to go, but not what to do once he got there. She said that an older and more experienced dog probably would have gone down to the rescue.

Castonguay had a few other interesting experiences while training her dogs. One day she sighted two girls in a motionless canoe fifty yards from shore who'd lost their paddles and, to make things more difficult, spoke almost no English.

Castonguay was readying Sunny for her Senior Water Dog certification and thought it a great chance to get in some on-the-job-training. Castonguay yelled to the girls, explaining that the dog

Newfoundlands keep a keen eye on anyone swimming.

would bring them a line and then tow them to shore, but the girls had no idea what she was saying and were scared to death of the big dog.

By coincidence, a man came along who could translate and after he had explained, the girls nodded in agreement. Sunny swam to the boat with the line but the girls refused to take it, as they couldn't bring themselves to get close to a dog of that size. Sunny, assuming they had the line, turned to begin the tow but stopped when she felt no weight on it. She took the line back to the canoe and, at a loss but set on doing her job, swam round it several times. Finally, when her back was turned, the girls steeled themselves and grabbed the line, and though the boat was strange and the people behaved in an unusual manner, Sunny performed as she had been trained. Even with disobliging "victims," she knew what to do.

Newfoundlands are excellent in the field of search-and-rescue because not only do they enjoy swimming, they are very good at it and most have no fear of water. Some breeds have to be trained in these basics.

While there are no official numbers on how many Newfoundlands are certified as water search-and-recovery dogs, Nicki Gundersen, owner of Calvin, who locates drowned victims, estimates there are fewer than fifty in the United States. She and her dog respond to several calls each year, mostly boating and swimming accidents.

In Lenexa, Kansas, where Gundersen and Calvin live, the dog's skills are especially useful, as lakes and rivers have silt bottoms and there is limited visibility in the murky water. Calvin reduces the search area for dive teams and dramatically shortens the time needed for a search.

Gundersen recalled a case where a man had been dared to swim across a turbulent river but didn't make it to the other side. The victim's family and park rangers searched eight hours for the man without success. Calvin was called in and it took him forty-five minutes to locate the body.

Surprisingly, at the scene of an accident Calvin doesn't leap into the water and search for the victim. Instead, the 125-pound dog rides in a small inflatable boat, sniffing the water's surface for gasses, oil, and skin particles that have risen to the surface. When Calvin picks up the scent, he barks once or twice and Gundersen concentrates on that area until Calvin scratches at the bottom of the boat, indicating he has found the victim. A dive team is then sent to retrieve the body.

In June 2004, the Life Network's television series *Dogs with Jobs* showcased Moby, an oddly marked, three-and-a-half-year-old Landseer. Moby is an essential part of California's Rapture Marine Expeditions' crew and accompanies their ship *Rapture* on its voyages. A kind of ocean-borne summer camp, *Rapture's* passengers, numbering around 150, are normally children who are unused to the sea. Director of the organization Scott McClung owns the dog and he explained on the program that if anyone gets in trouble, Moby is there at once. The dog rounds out the crew and

Two Newfoundlands enjoying the water.

plays an essential part in handling the children during fire drills, search-and-rescue, and in the water. He "alerts" instantly if there's a problem.

He's always on guard and needs little direction. The crew have come to trust and rely on him. Some children hide the fact they have a cramp in the water, but Moby can't be fooled. McClung believes his dog can detect chemical changes in a person's breath that indicate stress, as he checks each child when they are in the water. Anyone in trouble has only to grab his vest or his fur to be pulled immediately to safety.

When Moby first began his work, his instinct was to find everyone in the water and drag them out. Now that he's maturing, he's come to realize that some people and dogs can have fun when wet. His skills were proven before the camera: a swimmer indicated that he was in trouble, and Moby immediately sprang from the Zodiac and went to the rescue. Even training exercises are real to him and he takes his job, both in the water and on board, very seriously.

McClung said that his dog's abilities and diligence make him a very valuable asset. He's an important member of the crew and of McClung's family.

Chapter 14

Sporting Dog

Newfoundlands considers themselves sporting dogs whether or not their owners believe this to be the case. Adept at catching fish, they also like to hunt—not for the kill but for the thrill of fetching and helping out. Boating is a special treat, as is anything involving water. The dogs may enter a game of fetch, football, hockey, hopscotch, or anything else that looks like fun—even checkers, often despite the objections of other participants.

Not only are Newfoundlands skilled at catching fish, but they leave the fish unmarked and usually place them in a neat pile. They are probably the only dogs to fish somewhat routinely, at times to feed themselves, sometimes to help their fishing masters, and sometimes just for fun. Aaron Thomas first recorded the fishing skills of the Newfoundland more two hundred years ago:

> Sunday, May 25 [1794] These Animals here bear a more hardier aspect in general to what their same specie do in England, so much so that on a superficial view their kind does not appear the same. Their difference ariseth thus—in Newfoundland the Dogs commonly are their own caterers. They chiefly live on Fish and many of these sturdy race fish for themselves. It is no very uncommon thing to see one of these Dogs catch a Fish. Bitter hunger is their monitor and

as it presses upon them they go to the waterside and set on a Rock, keeping as good a lookout as a Cat ever did for a Mouse. The instant a Fish appears they plunge into the water and seldom come up without their prey. This is a wonderful property in these Animals, but it is as true as it is singular, for when Newfoundland was first discover'd these Dogs were found in a wild state, none of the savage Indians did they associate with.

—from Murray, *The Newfoundland Journal of Aaron Thomas*

We don't just have Thomas' word for it. Around 1825, a Newfoundland dog in England had a lawsuit brought against him and his owner. The case, Booth Chern reports in *The New Complete Newfoundland*, was called *The Earl of Tankerville v. a Dog*, the suit being brought by Charles A. Bennett, Earl of Tankerville. The dog in question was said to have been owned by the Earl of Home, who was probably the Earl of Marchmont in Scotland, whose surname was Home or, sometimes, Hume. In any event, the peer of the realm lost his case in the action that evolved because the dog had been catching so many salmon that the Earl's stream was in danger of becoming depopulated.

Nearly every day the dog took up his post at the gate of a small dam, where he deftly snatched the salmon from the water as they swam upstream to spawn. He was quite good at it according to the record, as it states: "He has been known to kill from twelve to twenty salmon in a morning." Apparently he had no real passion for salmon, as he didn't eat them but put them in a tidy pile, off to one side.

A decade or so later, while J. B. Jukes was wandering about Newfoundland, he wrote of a fishing dog. On September 28, 1839, he described the actions of Watch, one of the heroic dogs owned by George Harvey of Isle aux Morts:

> He sat on a projecting rock, beneath a fish flake, or stage, where the fish are laid to dry, watching the water, which had a depth of six or eight feet, and the bottom of which was white with fish-bones. On throwing a piece of codfish into the water, three or four heavy clumsy-looking fish, called in Newfoundland "sculpins," with great heads and mouths, and many spines about them, and generally about a foot long, would swim in to catch it. These he would "set" attentively, and the moment one turned his broadside to him, he darted down like a fish-hawk, and seldom came up without the fish in his mouth. As he caught them, he carried them regularly to a place a few yards off, where he laid them down; and

The sporting dog is always ready to fetch anything—especially from the water.

they told us that in the summer he would sometimes make a pile of fifty or sixty a day, just at that place. He never attempted to eat them, but seemed to be fishing purely for his own amusement. I watched him for about two hours; and when the fish did not come, I observed he once or twice put his right foot in the water, and paddled it about. This foot was white; and Harvey said he did it to "toll" or entice the fish; but whether it was for that specific reason, or merely a motion of impatience, I could not exactly decide. The whole proceeding struck me as remarkable, more especially as they said he had never been taught anything of the kind.

—from Jukes, *Excursions in and About Newfoundland*

After observing the customary practices of dogs like Watch, Reverend Philip Tocque was duly impressed by the abilities of those dogs carried in fishing boats. He mentions in his book *Newfoundland as it was and as it is in 1877* that "A dog is kept on board who is the daily companion of fishermen, and is so well-trained, that he immediately jumps into the water and secures the fish." Many Newfoundland inshore* fishermen, particularly along the southwest coast, took the dogs with them in their small boats. The dogs sat poised to fetch any fish that slipped from the hook and it was fairly common to see a Newfoundland at the gunwale of a fishing boat.

Always ready to snap at any fish in danger of escaping, they sometimes fetched the fish aboard with a paw. If one did succeed in getting off the hook, it wasn't unusual for the dog to follow it into the water and bring it back. One fisherman reported that his dog was particularly adept at recovering fish, and counted the number his shipmate had saved. He discovered his dog accounted for one-third of his catch.

The Newfoundland also makes an excellent hunting partner, and can always be relied on to act in a mature and responsible manner. Reverend G. G. Howse and some companions were hunting caribou near Terra Nova in the winter of 1910 and they took Captain along, whom Howse had raised from a pup. Harold MacPherson relates the story in *The Book of Newfoundland.*

One morning they tied their two dog teams up at their camp and left for the day. They had gone only a mile or so when one team, having broken free, caught up with them. The hunters had to return them to camp and when they arrived they found Captain preventing his teammates from chewing through their traces as well. Howse said he could always depend on the dog to guard his sled until he returned, and he would also take the empty vehicle home if told to do so.

Howse also recounted the preparations for a Labrador fishing voyage. A spring-balance that was on their schooner was needed, but the ship was anchored some four hundred yards offshore, and there was no boat available. They were in a quandary until Captain came by. Calling to a man on the schooner, Howse told him to give Captain the balance, then sent the dog for it. It took only a few minutes for him to swim to the vessel and return with the required item.

Later that summer, while sailing along the Labrador coast, the crew had the opportunity to supplement their diet with seabirds. Captain watched and waited until someone brought down one or more birds, then sprang over the side and fetched them back, often collecting as many as five or six at once.

Excelling as retrievers, especially when fetching birds from rough seas, Newfoundlands will leap from a boat and chase an injured duck beneath the water and over the ice until they capture it. Their soft mouth ensures the fowl will not be damaged and they have been known to catch a bird and release it unharmed.

Some years ago a Fogo Island merchant and passionate hunter told MacPherson how he and a friend took his Newfoundland dog one morning to hunt duck on the island. He also had a nine-month-old Newfoundland pup that, having escaped from his pen, caught up to them some miles farther along. It being too late to return him to his kennel, he fastened the pup's collar to the older dog's while they waited for the birds to show up.

When the birds finally put in an appearance, two volleys from the double-barrelled shotguns killed or wounded twenty-two. The dogs were released, the pup following the older, and both sprang into the water. They picked up as many birds as they could carry, then found they couldn't regain the shore because the ice formed a sheer two-foot barrier on the water. Hooking a gaff into the dogs' collars the hunters lifted them high enough to take the ducks from their mouths, then dropped them back into the water to retrieve others. Enthusiastically they brought back all the birds, the quick-learning pup fetching ten of them. The repeated "hangings" and immersions in the frigid water bothered them not in the least.

Bud Basola owned the 66,000 acre B-B buffalo ranch in Wyoming, where part of the NBC documentary of the Lewis and Clark expedition was filmed. Basola told Margaret Booth Chern that Hard Tack kept them entertained and they hated to part with him when it was over—so much so that they later acquired a Newfoundland of their own, Saki (Little Bear's Sacajawea), who learned the finer points of fetching game from their nine-year-old retriever. Basola said she retrieved doves with a very soft mouth and jumped into the back of the pickup truck without harming the birds. She shortly became an excellent retriever and was very proud of the work she did when taken on pheasant and turkey hunts. A year later Basola brought a young pointer home, and before much time had passed Saki had taught him to retrieve as well.

One final hunting story, which made the rounds in Newfoundland in the 1960s and is in all likelihood true, involves a hunter who missed five successive shots at ducks that his Newfoundland dog, Buck, had pointed. After the fifth miss, his dog disappeared but the hunter could hear him splashing about in the water and reeds. A few minutes later he returned with a live and uninjured duck in his mouth.

Evidently, fishing and hunting aren't the only sports of interest to Newfoundlands. No one knows the name of the dog who was obviously one of our earliest hockey fans. In 1905 the Stanley Cup series pitted Dawson City, Yukon Territory, against the reigning champions, the Ottawa Silver Seven. The game, played in Ottawa, was interrupted when the dog decided to take part in the game by rushing onto the ice, blocking a pass, then freezing the puck. The Ottawa team won the game twenty-eight to zero and vigorously denied that the dog had anything to do with the final score.

Football seems to be another preferred game for these dogs though perhaps other breeds would take it up if they could fit a football in their mouths. Bruce Terriberry told Booth Chern that his favourite dog as a child was Stormy (Ch. Far Horizon's Stormalong), the best football player around. The big dog's main concern was winning, and he could play guard or tackle and could carry the ball.

The Newfoundland is not deterred by ice or snow.

The author's own Chelsey could run with a regulation-sized football in her mouth, but a basketball was a little beyond her oral grasp. Charging onto the court, she would gather the ball between her front paws, place her chin on it, and run, followed by the shrieking and laughing children who wanted it back. The sheer size and willpower of the dog usually made this enterprise impossible.

Kevin Dixon and Lynne Park-Dixon of Belleville, Ontario, took their Newfoundland, Nemo, with them when engaged in outdoor activities. He rode in their canoe without tipping it, even taking a drink en route. When they went kayaking in winter Nemo swam beside them, the cold water seemingly having little effect on him.

And finally, Newfoundlands Steffi and Dory, also the author's, had their totally unexpected debut on television when they were filmed by *Outdoor Life*. Having swum out to meet two kayakers at Sandy

Cove in Bonavista Bay, they were unaware they were being filmed for posterity by those same kayakers! The dogs were a bonus for the cameraman, who found no icebergs or seals around. For some time afterward their baffled owners met people who exclaimed, "I saw those dogs on TV!"

Chapter 15

Animal Friends

Many, even those who own them, don't realize that Newfoundland dogs prefer to hang about with their immediate family and, in particular, with another Newfoundland in the same family. When two Newfoundlands who have never seen one another before are brought into the same house, they become exceptionally close friends in a very short time.

The dogs have proven that they are not only friendly toward other Newfoundlands and humans, but are congenial with almost any creature. If they dislike something, they ask only that it leave them alone. Numerous stories are told of the dogs and their often-curious chums.

Reverend F. O. Morris told Edwin Morris of the AKC Gazette in 1925 of the hatred between a Newfoundland and a mastiff at Donaghadee in northeast Ireland. No one knew the cause of the bad blood, but the pushy mastiff was suspected of being the instigator. Nearly every day they met somewhere in the small town, and nearly every day they quarrelled. One morning the fight began on a long mole projecting out into the North Channel. During the struggle both tumbled from the steep-sided jetty into the water, and there was no way to reach safety but by swimming the considerable distance to shore.

The Newfoundland swam to the beach with ease and, upon reaching the shore, shook the water from his coat then looked for his antagonist. He saw that the mastiff had worn himself out fighting the tide and waves and could barely keep his head above water. His recent adversary was on the verge of drowning when the Newfoundland shot from the beach like a horizontal jack-in-the-box. Cresting the heaving surf he grasped the other's collar and, holding his head out of the water, pulled him to shore.

The two never fought again and became inseparable friends, one seldom being seen unaccompanied by the other. Years later, the mastiff died in an accident and the Newfoundland was grief-stricken at the loss of his companion, mourning for days.

In 1798 General Henry Proctor was stationed at what is now Niagara-on-the-Lake, Ontario, during the construction of Fort George. He was accompanied by Neptune, his large Newfoundland dog. The soldiers there had tamed a fox and quartered it in a puncheon, tied by a long cord. Neptune soon discovered this interesting creature and visited it daily, becoming its good friend. On one of the general's informal inspections he approached the puncheon and, not seeing the fox, told one of the men their fox had run off. He kicked the supposedly vacant puncheon to make his point and the startled fox, having been inside her house all along, ran out in a panic, snapped the light tether, and disappeared into the forest.

Dory and Steffi are the best of friends.

The general sent Neptune to find his friend. In less than half an hour Neptune came back, tugging the protesting fox by the remaining piece of cord.

The soldiers praised and petted the dog and the general was so proud of him that on the next day he had the fox released again to show off his dog's astuteness. After a short search Neptune returned with his quarry once more, having had a great romp through the woods and fields.

From then on an unusual sort of fox hunt took place each day to the amusement of soldiers, dog, and, we hope, the fox.

Most dogs become very defensive in the presence of a much larger dog. When attacked by these insecure, discourteous, and short-tempered creatures, the poor Newfoundland seldom retaliates, but with a look of puzzled hurt on its face usually backs off, tail slowly waving. Sometimes Newfoundlands show their contempt by urinating on their tormentor but often, given time, they become fast friends.

Lord Byron lived at Newstead Abbey, near Nottingham, and his mother owned Gilpin, a fox terrier, that for some unknown reason held a profound grudge against Boatswain. The two dogs squabbled daily and the family feared the big dog would kill the pest. Finally, Byron's mother gave Gilpin to someone in the village of Newstead in hope of saving his life.

At about that same time Byron went to Cambridge and left his dog at home in the care of his servant. A few mornings later Boatswain could not be found and the frenzied servant searched high and low, to no avail. That evening the Newfoundland returned, followed by Gilpin, upon whom he lavished great attention.

It was learned that Boatswain had gone to Newstead, found his irritant, and brought him home. After that, any time Gilpin appeared to be in trouble his big friend quickly came to his assistance. And as far as we know, Boatswain never urinated on Gilpin.

Some animals do not return the overtures of a friendly Newfoundland. Nestor belonged to Captain Furneaux of the seal-hunting brigantine *Topaz*, and he was on board when J. B. Jukes accompanied that vessel to the ice in the spring of 1840.

Jukes relates in *Excursions in and About Newfoundland* that on March of that year Captain Furneaux announced that the first seal to be taken would earn the "swiler"* a quart of rum. With this sort of inspiration it wasn't long before a bedlamer* was brought on board. A curious Nestor, tail waving, approached the young seal without the least trepidation, and was bitten on the nose for his pains.

He was probably not a slow learner, just willing to forgive and forget, but on April 2 the inquisitive dog had another encounter with a seal, a young harp.* This time he spotted a seal in the water nearby, and jumped in to investigate. In the ensuing fracas he was badly bitten on the lip. The seal's head and body being so round, Nestor could not get a grip on anything but a flipper, and was forced to retreat.

Newfoundlands are natural protectors, not only of human children but commonly of baby animals as well. A tale of a dog and a lame puppy was told by Newfoundland aficionado and author of *The Dog*, William Youatt. When visiting a friend he and his Newfoundland approached a gate and found the puppy lying in front of it. The gate couldn't be opened without striking the puppy and possibly hurting it, and Youatt was about pick it up and move it to one side. To Youatt's surprise his dog put out a big paw and gently rolled the puppy out of the way, then stepped back to allow him open the gate.

Harold MacPherson had a fine dog, Bob (Westerland's Captain Bob Bartlett). One rain-drenched fall day the brook at Westerland turned into a virtual river. When a man left the farm to plough a field on the other side of the brook, a small terrier followed him and was swept away by the torrent. One-year-old Bob leapt into the water, swam to the terrier, who climbed onto his back, then returned to shore with his small acquaintance.

Sometimes other animals are not open to the Newfoundland's friendly overtures.

A great friendship sprang up between a Newfoundland and a St. Bernard at the huge World War Two allied air base at Gander, Newfoundland. At the end of the war the Americans and British pulled out of Gander and left their mascots behind because of quarantine regulations. Sandy, the Newfoundland, and Barry, the St. Bernard, were rather alike; both were friendly and weighed about 175 pounds. Rather than considering themselves abandoned, the two adopted the entire town, and the town them.

One would expect a rivalry between the two big males, but they were the best of friends and wandered the town indiscriminately, visiting any place that looked profitable. They were known and loved by everyone, and it wasn't unusual for the two behemoths to knock at a door, stroll into the kitchen, and flop down on the floor. While the children of the house patted and climbed over them, someone would fetch them food and water.

Sandy had the Newfoundland's predilection for lying in doorways. On a busy Saturday he could be found sprawled across the threshold of the Gander Co-op Store with patrons patiently climbing over him while Barry, lying off to one side, looked on. Both lived to a ripe old age, well into their teens, and were fast friends until they died.

At times even a Newfoundland can get in over its depth. Around 1920 columnist Peter Boggs wrote in Colorado's *New Haven Register* that one had taken the position of foster mother to care for some lambs. A sheep rancher's dog, she had lost her first litter of puppies, and when she discovered the orphaned lambs in a pen, she decided that she was responsible for feeding and cleaning the lambs and keeping them warm.

When the lambs had grown to the point where they could be put in the pasture, she accompanied her family and watched over it. Shortly, the rancher found she had been catching rabbits for her lambs and couldn't comprehend why the ungrateful wretches wouldn't eat them.

Hard Tack, star of the Lewis and Clark documentary, had better luck providing for his friends. He once pushed a litter of kittens aside and helped himself to their food. His owner turned around, saw what he had done, and scolded him. An aggrieved Hard Tack departed with his head down.

After the other dogs had been fed and his master was opening a can of fish for the kittens, Hard Tack appeared in the doorway with a catfish. He dropped the fish in front of the kittens and then sat down and proudly watched them eat.

Mildred Aiken had a very large and very gentle female Newfoundland, Dinah. After a bad storm she brought home a young Philadelphia vireo that had been blown from its nest. They cared for the unfledged bird until it was ready to fly, the mother bird coming to feed it every day, much to the delight of Dinah and the neighbourhood children. Neither bird had any fear of the dog, who wanted no one but Aiken to handle the nestling.

Dinah acted similarly with a litter of kittens. Aiken could handle them and members of the family could look at them, but others were kept away. If anyone attempted to touch the kittens, Dinah took their hands in her mouth and pulled them aside.

When four-year-old Chelsey was brought home, having been rescued from an abusive owner, she was closely watched when outside her enclosure, not least of all by Boatswain, another Newfoundland in the family

Clyde the cat has survived the arrival of five full-grown Newfoundlands.

(of the author). Boatswain was accustomed to sitting at the end of the driveway, greeting children as they passed by on their way to and from school. Chelsey once saw an opportunity to escape and dashed for the busy street, her new owner shouting at her to come back. Boatswain leapt to his feet, roared at her and blocked her way. She froze and he escorted her back to the front steps, then returned to his post. Gradually, over a period of weeks, he allowed her to sit with him—but always a little to the rear. When Boatswain walked with Chelsey he insisted on carrying her leash. It made little difference if his leash was untended, he retained his hold on hers and she compliantly ambled along beside him.

Boatswain eventually died and Umbra was rescued. Chelsey took over as instructor and taught him exactly what she had learned earlier from Boatswain. She also taught three puppies, Jake, Chimo, and Smudge, the rules of the house.

S. J. Navin's Nanahboozoo (Can. Ch. Nanahboozoo of Stevens) was a huge dog, more than thirty-four inches tall at the shoulder and nearly thirty-five inches long. He was reared in the Canadian woods, where he became acquainted with a tribe most dangerous to dogs— the porcupine. Booth Chern's *The New Complete Newfoundland* contains the remarkable story.

A particular porcupine became one of his close friends, and Nanahboozoo met him each day to stroll along a trail. His bristly buddy usually led and the dog followed, sometimes even prodding his little buddy to move faster. One day a "sportsman" shot the porcupine, and when Nanahboozoo arrived he found his friend lying lifeless on the trail. Navin said the big dog sat down beside his friend and cried.

Silver Flute was in a class by herself. John Gibbons of Tennessee owned her and she in turn had her own pets: tropical fish. Having adopted the family's aquarium, she was captivated by its contents. She spent hours watching them and when there was a change in the number of fish inhabiting the tank, she became very excited, pulling members of the family over to see any new arrivals. She never failed to take visitors to see her fish. Those who called frequently were usually shown only once, but after a significant interval of time between visits, she proudly escorted them in to view her pets again.

Chapter 16

What a Dog!

Many Newfoundlands have had no opportunity to prove they have the stuff of heroes, escape artists, or slapstick comedians. Sensitivity and the ability to understand the more subtle aspects of their masters' speech and more abstract matters seem to distinguish the breed, and we must not overlook them.

That Newfoundlands have a definite sense of humour should not pass unnoticed either. They take an obscure delight in practising upon us humans and other animals of lower orders. Their dignity, like that of all Newfoundlanders, is a cloak to take off or put on as the occasion requires.

Around 1950, eight-year-old Winston Hollett of Norris Arm, Newfoundland, had a dog named Buff. During the winter he was often harnessed to a light sled and he ran like the wind, when he felt like it. Once, when the boy was trying to encourage a recalcitrant Buff to resume his running he shouted, "Get on, Buff! Get on!" Whereupon Buff slowly walked back to the sled, climbed on and sat down.

The Newfoundland's sense of humour has provided fodder for a few writers and artists. The comic strip *Napoleon*, created by Clifford McBride, was featured in the *New York Sun* beginning in 1929. Its lead characters were the dog Napoleon and his owner, Uncle Elby, based on McBride's own uncle, Elby Eastman, and his dog.

To begin with, Napoleon was a large, black-and-white mongrel, but he was later replaced by a St. Bernard. The latter was succeeded by Rollo (Flintridge Rollo), a Newfoundland well-known in the community of Pasadena, California, where he took part in the Rose Bowl Parade each year. He loved to meet people and was reputedly very entertaining. Most of McBride's later works, and those of artists who took over for him after his death, were based on Rollo's antics until the strip was dropped in 1960.

The *Spy and Christian Citizen* of Worcester, Massachusetts, printed this story of Tige in the 1850s:

> Tige was a splendid Newfoundland, and possessed good sense as well as good looks. He was in the habit of going every morning with a penny in his mouth, to the same butcher's shop, and purchasing his own breakfast, like a gentlemanly dog as he was. But it so happened upon one cold morning, during the winter, the shop was closed, and the necessity seemed to be imposed upon Tige, either to wait for the butcher's return, or look for his breakfast elsewhere. Hunger probably constrained him to take the latter alternative, and off he started for another butcher's shop, nearest to his favourite place of resort. Arriving there, he deposited his money upon the block, and smacked his chops for breakfast as usual; but the butcher, instead of meeting the demand of his customer as a gentleman might, brushed the coin into his till, and drove the dog out of the shop. Such a disgraceful proceeding on the part of a man, very naturally ruffled the temper of the brute; but as there was not other alternative, he was obliged

to submit. The next morn-
ing, however, when his
master furnished him with
the coin for the purchase
of breakfast, as usual, the
dog instead of going to
the shop where he had
been accustomed to trade,
went immediately to the
shop from whence he
was so unceremoniously
ejected the day before—
laid his penny upon the
block, and with a growl,
as much as to say, 'you
don't play any more tricks
upon travellers,' placed his
paw upon the penny. The

Clifford McBride's *Napoleon* featured the
antics of the Newfoundland Rollo.

butcher, not liking to risk, under such a demonstration, the
perpetration of another fraud, immediately rendered him the
quid pro quo, in the shape of a slice of meat, and was about
to appropriate the penny as he had done the day previous, to
his own coffers; but the dog, quicker than he was, made away
with the meat at one swallow, and seizing the penny again in
his mouth, made off to the shop of his more honest acquaintance, and by the purchase of a double breakfast, made up for
his previous fast.

    —quoted in Tocque,
    Newfoundland as it was and as it is in 1877

Dandie, a Newfoundland owned by a well-to-do Mr. M'Intyre in Scotland, was a dog to be reckoned with. M. Drury's book *This is the Newfoundland* records numerous stories about the immensely clever dog.

Some of M'Intyre's friends were greatly amused by Dandie and each day gave him a penny so he could visit the local baker and buy a roll. One day he met one of the men and waited expectantly for his roll money. His acquaintance told him that he had none with him but did at home. Having all but forgotten the incident, the man returned home and shortly afterward heard a noise at the door. When he opened it, Dandie ambled in, looking for his penny. As a miserable sort of joke the man gave him a substitute that looked like a penny and poor Dandie went off to see the baker. The baker, obviously a skinflint, turned him down flat.

Dandie took the counterfeit and went back to the man's house, where he scratched at the door. The door was opened and he walked in, dropped the penny at the man's feet, then scornfully walked off.

Usually Dandie spent his money as soon as it was given to him but he had more business acumen than many people. One day when he had not, to anyone's knowledge, been given a penny, he brought home a roll. Curious, next day M'Intyre followed Dandie into a bedroom and watched him rummage around beneath a bed, but when Dandie realized his owner was snooping, he stopped. M'Intyre restrained the dog, who resisted and grumbled, while his maid looked beneath the bed. There she found seven halfpence covered with a cloth. Dandie immediately changed his hiding place to the backyard, beneath a pile of sawdust.

M'Intyre always had visitors and they expected to be entertained by Dandie, who performed some impressive tricks. One of his tricks was to find a designated card from a deck that had been scattered around a room. He seldom failed.

M'Intyre sometimes hid a comb for him to find and, to make it more difficult, he placed other personal articles about the room. When Dandie was let back in and ordered to find the comb, he had little difficulty in ignoring the other items, locating the comb almost at once and taking it to his master. Since M'Intyre had touched all the objects, the dog could not have been relying on scent, but the wording of his instructions.

If Dandie wanted to enter the house, he pulled the bell rope and uncomplainingly waited for the door to be opened. When he wanted to enter another room and the door was closed, he took advantage of the hand bell used to call the servants and shook it vigorously.

A guest once dropped a shilling on the floor and no one could find it. M'Intyre noticed Dandie sitting off to one side, apparently paying no attention at all to the event. He called his dog over and told him that if he could find the shilling he'd be given a biscuit. Dandie walked over to the table and placed on it the coin that he'd earlier picked up, unobserved.

In 1869 James Howley, dedicated geological and topographical surveyor and advocate of developing Newfoundland's natural wealth, was travelling about the island in search of minerals of value. He recounted events at one of his fact-finding sites:

> Our next point for examination was Pitt Sound Island in the entrance to Bloody Bay Reach, locally known as the Cow

Path. Here in a small cove called Beaver Cove, Mr. M Carroll with a few men were engaged in sinking a shaft upon a small deposit of copper which we were asked to examine…Here Mr. Carroll had erected a log tilt* in which he and his men resided. He was a queer genius of a man, and afforded us much amusement by his quaint yarns and sayings. He had four or five magnificent Newfoundland dogs with him, about the finest specimens I ever saw. They were coal-black, sleek and well-fed…Carroll often entertained us with a series of comic exhibitions greatly to our amusement. He would call the dogs to him and give them certain orders. They would sit on their haunches, while Carroll stood on one side. Throwing a piece of bread or meat on the ground in the centre of the circle, he would then strike an attitude, fold his arms and with head in air commence to whistle a medley of airs while the dogs with eyes intently fixed on the food listened motionless, not daring to budge until he glided off into some familiar air previously announced by him as the signal of release. The moment he uttered the first bar of this particular tune the dogs would make a headlong rush for the morsel of food. He sometimes varied this performance by pointing to some individual in the group and saying, "When I take off his hat you can have the bread." He would then walk around from one to another, the dogs watching him intently but not daring to budge till he approached the individual in question and removed his hat, then again the dogs would make their dive.

—from Howley, *Reminiscences of James P. Howley*

The dogs have become well accustomed to the vagaries of their two-legged friends. C. A. Richardson, sister-in-law of William Richardson, President Grant's Secretary of the Treasury in 1873, owned a sizeable Newfoundland, Caesar. She took her children and dog to a daguerreotypist in Lowell, Massachusetts, for a group picture.

She tried to get the children and dog to sit still but before the shutter could be closed one of the subjects, usually the dog, moved. Eventually, after an hour or so of frustration, she angrily ordered the dog to go home. A chastened Caesar put his tail down and dejectedly slipped out the door.

The next day, to his mistress' astonishment, Caesar came home with a box hung around his neck. With a self-satisfied air he waited expectantly while she opened it. She found it contained a daguerreotype of the dog. The owner of the studio explained that a short time after they had left, the dog had returned and demanded to be let in. By his actions he convinced the owner that he had come back to have his picture taken.

Newfoundlands prefer to remain with their friends and are not prone to running away. Nevertheless, the breed has produced more than its share of escape artists. One summer, fed up with unrestrained dogs harassing residents and fouling public property, the mayor of Plymouth, England, ordered that all dogs found running free were to be picked up and tied in the prison yard. Among those gathered in was an adventurous Newfoundland dog from a ship newly arrived in port.

Taken into custody and placed in the prison yard, he quickly chewed through his tether and, heeding the cries of his fellow prisoners, released three of the four of them before the breakout was terminated by the return of the jailer.

Margaret Booth Chern's Race, she reports in *The New Complete Newfoundland,* had been escaping from a six-foot-high chain-link-fenced pen. No one ever saw him get out and they doubted that he jumped over the fench. Not yet completely grown, he had never been seen to jump anything approaching that height. Yet no holes were found in or under the fence, though a small stream ran through the pen. The gate, with its dog-proof catch, was always closed, but still Race would show up on the front steps or be seen peeking in through a window.

Someone eventually noticed that Race's chest and legs were wet, but his escape route still wasn't clear. The water came in through a pipe, far too small for a Newfoundland to fit into, and it ran out through a wooden grate. In any event, the grate was taken out and a discarded Christmas tree was jammed into the opening to ensure escape by that avenue was impossible, but the dog continued to appear unexpectedly in odd places.

Around New Year's there was a heavy snowfall, and when Race appeared at the door his owners checked out the pen immediately. The gate was still locked and the Christmas tree in place, but paw prints bore witness to Race's furtiveness. He had taken the tree out and pushed it back to hide his getaway. Race was taken into the house until a witness could be found to verify the tale told by the tracks.

The author's Umbra had never to anyone's knowledge opened a gate, but it seems the necessity had simply never arisen. It became essential on the day Jake, a Rhodesian ridgeback, visited. Chelsey had known Jake since he was a puppy, but Umbra had never made his acquaintance; thus, while Chelsey was allowed to associate with Jake on the front lawn, Umbra was confined to the yard. The aggressive Jake growled at Chelsey, and Umbra's paw flashed up and unlatched the gate, and he rushed out to join the fray.

Newfoundlands also have a devious side that is belied by the expression of innocence they habitually present. An incident that occurred on Newfoundland's south shore in the 1930s will serve to show this side of their character. In this case our heroic dog was loafing on the government wharf when a little girl playing there fell into the deep water.

Elerted by her screams, our valiant Newfoundland plunged from the wharf, located the child in the dark water, and dragged her to shore, where her frantic mother, who had also heard the cries, caught her up. A great fuss was made over the wonderful dog and he was given treats, petted and praised. From that day on the dog patrolled the wharf diligently and children were no longer safe there. Longing to relive his day of glory, the dog rescued each and every boy or girl who happened along—after he had pushed them into the water.

Boatswain at a favourite game: "Come get your hat!"

When Amber Fortier's Mauzy visited Boatswain's household,

she invariably picked up a rawhide and chewed on it for a while. When it was time to go home, she obediently went to the car and climbed in. Only after they had been home for some time after one visit did her owner discover she had filched a rawhide chew. After three or four occurrences Mauzy was frisked before she left the house and nine times out of ten she had a rawhide or a ball. When she had filched some object, she was studiously insouciant and avoided eye contact, keeping her normally open mouth tightly shut.

Megan Nutbeem tells in *The Book of Newfoundland* of the retrieving habits of one Tarmac. She, with her husband Bob and their four children, took the one-year-old dog with them when they visited the beach at Bristols Hope, Newfoundland:

> Bob and the children decided to go wading, and I lay on the beach half asleep. Christopher had left his shoes too near the edge of the water, and when the tide crept in his shoe started out to sea. Bob, who was up the beach, called to one of our daughters to get the shoe. She didn't hear him, but Tarmac did. Out he swam, retrieved the shoe, and returned to have a great fuss made of him by all of us. He then brought the mate up from the beach, and again was told how smart he was, how very clever, a marvellous fellow. Then I dozed off, and the others returned to their fun in the water. All of a sudden I felt something was just not normal, and when I looked beside me there was a pile of shoes—red ones, blue ones, white ones and black ones, men's women's and children's! And there was my honourable Tarmac coming up the beach with two sneakers in his mouth—and he was so pleased with himself. Fortunately,

all the people on the beach thought it was a howling scream, and we spent the rest of the afternoon trotting up and down delivering the right shoes to the real owners.

—Smallwood, *The Book of Newfoundland*

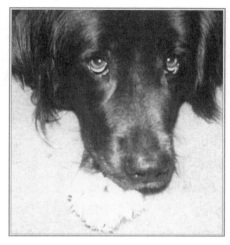

Steel-grey Mauzy, quite the trickster.

While no recommendation is made that you watch the 1985 comedy movie *Police Academy II*, if you do have the opportunity to see it you will notice the large bronze Newfoundland, Kodiak, who played Lou, the dog. Kodiak was the most titled Newfoundland in the breed's history at the time, and he also had roles in a number of television shows.

It was said that he developed a swelled head during his acting career and began to ignore directors, sometimes even walking off the set if he felt there were too many retakes. This is not unusual among stars who are gravely put upon by arrogant directors and demanding technicians. (Still, like most Newfoundlands, he knew what was really important. He became a real-life hero when he saved his mistress from a smoke-filled house.)

At times these "wonder dogs" have erred. The *Union Leader & New Hampshire Sunday News* of December 21, 2002, reports that the day before, just after 4:30 a.m., a ten-wheel trash compactor truck smashed through the guardrails on Adams Street in the Mascenic area of Greenville, New Hampshire. It landed nose-first in the Sougegan River below, and behind the wheel, unhurt and nonchalant, was the furry, four-footed culprit. Man's best friend had wrecked man's ten-wheeler.

Three-year-old Bear didn't want to be left alone in the cab when Glen Shaw went to empty trash cans into the back of his truck. Shaw said that as he was picking up garbage near the intersection of Adams Street and River Road the truck began rolling toward the river "in slow motion." As it gathered momentum, he was left behind to watch his vehicle plunge into the water.

Shaw, who had to go into the river to rescue Bear, said his dog had somehow contrived to release the hand brake. A hazardous-materials team was called in from Nashua to contain a fuel leak and was there for two hours, according to acting police chief Larry Duval. Ann Shaw, Glen's wife and co-owner of the business, told reporters, "My husband said that's [Bear's] last ride in the truck."

Chapter 17

Worldwide Recognition

The Newfoundland is recognized all over the world today. Many honours other than those for heroic deeds have been heaped upon our dog.

In Nashville, Tennessee, there's a statue of a Newfoundland dog who, apparently, did nothing but be a Newfoundland dog. Perhaps it was erected in honour of the entire breed. It's on the grounds of Belmont University, part of the original Belmont mansion built by Joseph and Adelicia Acklen in 1853. The residence was once surrounded by splendid gardens with an assortment of gazebos and statues, a deer park, a bear house, a zoo, and an artificial lake complete with alligators.

No one has any recollection of a Newfoundland ever having lived on the estate, but Adelicia is known to have had statues of creatures she'd never owned. No one can blame her for admiring the form of our breed!

Perhaps because of its lordly demeanour, the Newfoundland has been a natural choice for royalty. His Royal Highness the Prince of Wales, the future Edward VII, arrived at St. John's on July 4, 1860, to begin a tour of North America. He was received by Governor Sir Alexander Bannerman, and a guard of honour formed by the Newfoundland Corps, and was escorted to Government House in a long and splendid procession.

After a tour around Quidi Vidi Lake during the St. John's Regatta the next day, according to Charles Pedley's *History of Newfoundland*, a "noble Newfoundland dog was presented to the Prince by Chief Justice Sir Francis Brady, on behalf of the people of the Colony." Brady thought "Avalon" would be a good name for the dog, but Prince Edward thought differently. Because Avalon represented only the southeastern part of the Colony, he diplomatically called him Cabot. A fine specimen, Cabot had been raised by well-known dog fancier Bartholomew "Bat" Sullivan, who lived near Signal Hill in St. John's.

Cabot's silver collar was made by Tiffany's of New York and had two shields bearing the royal arms mounted on it, with a third shield between them inscribed "Presented to His Royal Highness Albert Edward Prince of Wales, by the inhabitants of Newfoundland, A.D. 1860."

This statue from the early nineteenth century resides in Williamstown, Massachusetts, and is identical to the Belmont University statue.

Reverend Charles Pedley observed: "He [the prince] showed a youthful joyousness, as well as a princely satisfaction, in accepting the gift of the citizens a noble Newfoundland dog, and instantly gave him the name of Cabot, in honour of the discoverer of the island."

Sullivan, however, had charged what was thought to be an exorbitant price for Cabot, and he wasn't paid. He sued the Prince of Wales for the balance due, in what became the celebrated "Batty" Sullivan dog case.

With the breed slowly disappearing from the island, Harold MacPherson, as reported by F. Galgay and M. McCarthy in *Olde St. John's*, told of the difficulty in securing a fitting gift for the Duke and Duchess of Cornwall and York (later the Prince and Princess of Wales, and still later King George V and Queen Mary) when they visited Newfoundland in 1901.

Seventeen years old at the time, MacPherson helped in the search for a Newfoundland dog and voiced his disappointment at the few moderately good ones to be found. The committee, in the hope that they would give something that would amuse the children of the royal household, found the best dog available and had a cart especially made for him by Oke's Carriage Factory of St John's.

The following year an advertisement for that company described the gift; dog-carting aficionados take note:

> Among the testimonials received by the Duke and Duchess (now Prince and Princess of Wales) during their Canadian tour in 1901, there was none more highly appreciated than that presented to them by 4000 children of Newfoundland, for their royal children. It was a Newfoundland dog, cart and harness. The cart, which was made by Mr. J. C. Oke was a creditable specimen of native workmanship. It was six feet long from tip of shaft to back of wheel, two and a half feet long in the body and built of oak, with hickory shafts, and lined with blue silk velvet. All the springs and other fittings were nickel and silver-plated. The wheels were of the ball-bearing bicycle style, with solid rubber tires. The seat was spring-cushioned.
>
> —from Galgay and McCarthy, *Olde St. John's*

After the formal presentation Her Royal Highness went to the dog, patted him, and examined him, then exclaimed, "Isn't he a beauty!" The committee was taken aback when the dog's handler blurted proudly, "Be gobs, Ma'am, 'e is. Ye won't foind the loikes of 'im nowhere." (Also from *Olde St. John's*.)

Either contributing to or because of its popularity, the Newfoundland has appeared on postage stamps all over the world. It was the first dog to be enshrined on any stamp, a distinction was fittingly conferred by Newfoundland's Colonial Government in 1887. The half-

Photo used in a 1906 advertisement for Oke's of St. John's, builder of the carriage presented to the Duke and Duchess of Cornwall.

cent stamp bore a three-quarter view of the dog's head based on Edwin Landseer's painting *A Distinguished Member of the Humane Society*. This portrait was redrawn by Sir Augustus John and was later used for the half-cent stamps, printed variously in red, orange, and black in that year and in 1898.

From 1932 to 1937, Newfoundland issued a fourteen-cent stamp with a full portrait of Sieger (who protected the nurse in trouble). In 1937 the same portrait was used on the stamp celebrating the coronation of King George VI, probably the only time a dog has shared a stamp with a monarch. The 1932–1937 version was reissued between 1941 and 1944 and used throughout the British Commonwealth.

Newfoundland's neighbours, the French islands of St. Pierre and Miquelon, issued a tax stamp with a full portrait of a Newfoundland on it in 1922. The islands produced postage stamps in various denominations from 1938 to 1940 depicting a team of the dogs. They were overprinted and used by the Free French government during World War Two.

In 1957 the French islands produced an airmail stamp bearing a Newfoundland's likeness and, in 1973, another tax stamp. Paraguay created a stamp showing a Newfoundland's head in 1986.

To celebrate the centennial of the CKC in 1988, Canada Post issued a set of four thirty-seven-cent se-tenant stamps

The half-cent stamp of 1887.

(stamps of different designs, colours, or values, printed side by side) commemorating native Canadian breeds, one of which was the Newfoundland as portrayed by renowned Canadian painter of dogs, Mia Lane.

Sieger's stamp from the 1930s.

At Christmas 1991, Great Britain's island of Jersey issued a set of Peter Pan stamps, one of which bore the likeness of the Darlings' Landseer, Nana. Monaco, in 1993, printed a stamp with a full side view of a Newfoundland, and there were also some Russian overprints with the dog on them, one from 1994. Tanzania produced a striking Newfoundland dog stamp in 1993.

Another Landseer appeared on Sierra Leone's stamp commemorating the 125th Anniversary of the Metropolitan Museum of Art,

A 1937 commemorative stamp honouring the coronation of King George VI.

in 1995; the dog is prominent in Renoir's *Madame Charpentier and her children*. About the same time Uganda printed a stamp showing a Newfoundland either diving into the water to save someone or diving in to swim with a pal.

In 1996 Mali, another country where you would not expect to encounter one of the dogs, issued a mini-sheet of which one stamp shows a Landseer swimming to a vessel in distress with a lifeline. The year 1997 was a good year for Newfoundland

Tanzania's 1993 stamp.

This handsome portrait of a Landseer is on the 1889 ten-dollar note of the Union Bank of Newfoundland.

A sterling silver coin featuring a sterling canine.

ance on a coin. The Royal Canadian Mint produced a fifty-cent collector's coin of sterling silver, bearing a Newfoundland's portrait.

Newfoundlands have been owned by many famous people other than those previously mentioned. Among proud Newfoundland dog–lovers have been such notables as George Washington, Humphrey Bogart, Robert Frost, Benjamin Franklin, Stephen Leacock, King Edward VII, and Queen Victoria. Ulysses S. Grant owned Faithful, and Bing Crosby began breeding Newfoundlands in the 1940s, then gave President Franklin Delano Roosevelt one of his puppies as a gift for the children of the Warm Springs Foundation. Robert Kennedy's Brumis was a celebrity in and around Washington, and Kennedy had a series of Newfoundlands afterward, primarily from Little Bear Kennels. Shania Twain is the proud owner of two of the brown variety.

Chapter 18

Show Dog and Competitor

Dog shows have a rigid caste system, and when a Newfoundland places behind a dog of a lesser breed, fans become incensed because the judge "picked that mere apology for a dog over the real thing!" The predilection of judges to select what some think of as diminutive, primped toys as best of show is almost more than the Newfoundland devotee can bear.

Fortunately, many judges recognize the superb form of the Newfoundland, and the breed often wins at shows. Only a few of the great Newfoundland champions will be mentioned here, as most of the winners would not be familiar to those outside the community of Newfoundland dog breeders and owners.

One of the greatest in the Newfoundland line was the English Siki. Born in 1922, he rose to become the most famous show and stud dog of the breed. He was the ideal of the day and through his descendants, there and in North America, determined a large percentage of the traits we prize in our dogs of today. Most champion Newfoundlands carry Siki's blood in their veins and, while he was not the dog exemplar, he

The famous Siki, father of champions.

nevertheless effectively combined the physical attributes, strength, flair, and disposition of the old Newfoundlands and the new.

Newton, bred by Harold MacPherson and acquired by New Yorker Mel Sokolsky, was by 1968 the top show dog among Newfoundlands, having won best-of-shows 15 times, best of the working group 55 times (placing among the top three an additional 138 times), best of specialty 8 times, and best of the breed a whopping 199 times. His performance provided an all-important boost to the interest in the Newfoundland.

Newfeld's Long John Silver, the first Newfoundland to become Canada's top show dog, won Toronto's Metropolitan Kennel Club's best-of-show in 1978. Longer and heavier than the standard, the big Landseer's gait had less of a roll than most Newfoundlands'; and he seemed to float along. He acquired his name because he had one black leg and, despite his odd markings, gait, and size, his comportment had everyone cheering for what many judges called the most beautiful dog they had ever seen.

Josh (Ch. Darbydale's All Rise Pouchcove), a large black dog, was born in 1999. Four years later he won best-of-breed and placed first in the working group at what is arguably the world's most prestigious dog show, the Westminster Kennel Club Dog Show at Madison Square Garden in New York. The 155-pound Josh, jointly owned by Peggy and David Helming and Carol Bernard Bergmann, was obviously their pride and joy.

Helming was thrilled and explained to Amy Satkofsky of the Pennsylvania *Express-Times* (February 13, 2003), "What was really great was watching people respond to him in the ring. Josh is just a big fuzzy teddy bear, and he has a great personality. It makes us proud that people can see that; that he can make people feel good."

During the working group judging, Josh basked in the crowd's adoration and watched himself on the big-screen scoreboard.

"You can tell he loves attention," Helming laughed, "and his personality at home is not much different than in the ring—he loves people."

At the following year's Westminster Show, on February 10, 2004, Josh won best-of-show against 2500 dogs of 162 breeds. Put through his paces by Michelle Ostermiller, he impressed Judge Burton Yamada as much as he did the crowd. He appeared on *The Late Show with David Letterman* and on *Good Morning America*. Practically every Newfoundlander saw the show or its results and all cheered for Josh.

Apart from run-of-the-mill dog shows, there are many competitions the Newfoundland can enter. The breed does well in all of them. Sanctioned dog agility competitions were developed in England in 1978 to break the Crufts Dog Shows into segments that would allow time to prepare for the next judging. These short competitions were vastly entertaining to the crowds, who were rivetted by dogs jumping fences, racing through tunnels, weaving between a series of poles, and getting past other obstructions. The contests caught on quickly and soon spread throughout the world.

It's amusing to see the expressions of those spectators who do not know the Newfoundland well when one is present at these events. To the astonishment of the crowd, a seemingly ponderous Newfoundland won the competition against its more agile-looking contenders around 1996.

One contest sponsored by Newfoundland dog clubs is the draught test. The first for the breed was held in the mid-1980s, and owners

Leonidas Hubbard's Moose exhibiting the qualities of a good draught dog c.1902.

were quick to embrace the re-enactment of this historic activity. The Newfoundland has a natural gift for the work.

To pass the test the unleashed dog has to come on call, stay, and co-operate while being harnessed and hitched to a cart. It must respond to the basic commands of "haul forward," "haul slowly," "stop," and "back up," and pull the cart through a difficult course. In doing so the dog overcomes such obstacles as a high narrow tunnel and a low narrow tunnel, negotiate tight ninety-degree turns, and execute patterns, like figure eights.

As part of a group, the dog has to haul a weighted cart over varied terrain for a mile, guided only by verbal commands and hand signals. The dogs have to work without a lead and, in spite of distractions, respond promptly to quiet commands. Above all, each dog and handler must demonstrate teamwork.

Draught competitions have become fairly common, and are among the more exciting exhibitions in today's dog world. Unfortunately, many dogs today, including the Newfoundland, have been bred to such an exceedingly fine standard that they cannot fulfill their original purpose. Indeed, many cannot live in comfort because of resultant physical or psychological problems. Megan Nutbeem's thoughts:

> Standards were originally derived from the jobs each breed was meant to do—for example Newfoundland dogs, originally draft dogs, needed heavy shoulders and strong backs in order to pull loads of wood. But the pursuit of the perfect

standard has led to dogs that seem like grotesque parodies of their working ancestors. By trying to breed dogs to fit the physical appearance of the best working dog, humans have created dogs whose deformed physiques would never allow them to work.

—from Smallwood, *The Book of Newfoundland*

Still, the Newfoundland seems to be holding its own reasonably well. Barbara Wolman's eight-year-old Nana (Ch. Barbara-Allen's Nana), weighing in at 148 pounds, set the female weight-hauling record for dogs at the Northwest Newfoundland Club Working Trials in 1973.

That same year, 162-pound Bonzo Bear pulled nearly 4300 pounds over the prescribed distance of fifteen feet in less than ninety seconds, at that point the heaviest load hauled by a dog ever recorded.

A St. Bernard, Ryette's Brandy Bear broke the record in 1978 at Bothell, Washington, when he pulled an amazing 6400 pounds— 36 pounds per pound of his 176-pound body weight. However, the strongest dog in the world, pound for pound, was the one-year-old, 97-pound Hans (Barbara-Allens Dark Hans). On July 20, 1979, he pulled 5045 pounds—52 pounds per pound of body weight. Hans was owned by Terri Dickinson of Kenmore, Washington. *The Guinness Book of World Records* has stopped listing the record, likely because participation in weight-hauling competitions has caused injury to some animals.

Not surprisingly, the Newfoundland also excels in tests for water dogs. Such a test was begun in England in the 1800s, but lapsed and was all but forgotten for years. It was finally revived there in

1965 and was brought to North America in 1973. The water trials consist of the six individual tests a dog must pass to be rated as a Water Rescue Dog.

The junior division is for beginners working toward the title of Water Dog. After passing this they are eligible for the senior division trials and the certificate proclaiming them Water Rescue Dogs.

The beginner's test is meant to examine whether the dog is dependable on land and responsive to its handler's voice commands or hand signals the first time they are given. The dog works through heeling, coming on call, and lying down and remaining in position for one minute. Dogs learn to fetch and deliver a life jacket, boat cushion, lifeline, or any number of articles. Of course, this also shows the handler has control of the dog. The other tests involved are described in detail in Chapter 13.

The Newfoundland, as we have seen, has wonderful potential as a companion dog, but there it must undergo rigorous trials in order to be accredited as such. A dog the size of a Newfoundland must have manners. Walking without pulling on the leash, sitting, lying down, or staying put when told to do so, coming when called, and politely greeting others are all crucial for a companion dog. When taught with love, fairness and consistency, a Newfoundland can become the best of household chums.

The AKC established obedience trials in the 1930s. The purpose of the competition is to ascertain dogs' ability to obey specific commands and to complete certain tasks. There are three classes of increasing difficulty, and there are four obedience titles to be won. Companion Dog (CD) is awarded to a dog in the novice class; Companion Dog Excellent (CDX), to a dog in the open class; Utility

Dog (UD), to a dog in the utility class; and Obedience Trial Champion (OTCH), which is awarded to a dog that has already won in the utility class.Competitions consist of high and broad jumps, retrieving, scent discrimination, and various commands for everyday use, such as "stay," "sit," "fetch," and so on. Standardized exercises are judged and scored, with deductions for major infractions. A dog must score at least 170 points or more out of a possible 200, without any zeroes along the way, to earn a "leg." To earn an obedience title a dog must earn a leg at three different shows.

The Newfoundland is also great at tracking, the sporting form of search-and-rescue. Scenting ability and enthusiasm for work are genetic in origin, but a dog must prove it can track before being allowed to enter a tracking test. A certification test, of a complexity equivalent to the Tracking Dog test, is administered. If the dog doesn't pass the certification test, it will not be allowed to compete for a Tracking Dog title.

To earn a basic title, the dog must follow a scent that's about half an hour old. The individual leaving the scent, a stranger to the dog, must walk a course, making curves and angles along the way. At the end of the trail the "scenter" leaves a glove that, of course, carries his or her scent. The dog, working in harness on a forty-foot lead, must follow the track without any help from the handler and find the glove.

This is the one sport where the dog must do all the work—a good thing, too, since a Newfoundland's nose is much better at identifying, sorting out, and following a scent than its human companion's.

Chapter 19

The Rescued

If we create a law making mandatory the licensing of dog owners, rather than the licensing of dogs, we would be doing a great
thing. Unfortunately, despite centuries of abuse to dogs, there has
been little progress on this front.

In the 1800s many admitted that the dogs were an important
part of Newfoundland's economy; nonetheless, while their work
was considered important the dogs in most cases were not. The ap-
palling way in which Newfoundlands were forced to work should
have weighed heavily on the consciences of their owners, but apparently the milk of human kindness dried up in Newfoundland
for many years.

All winter the dogs worked alone and in teams hauling fish,
firewood, lumber, and merchandise. One of these powerful and essential animals could maintain a household through the winter by
its labours. When the summer fishing season arrived, however, the
dogs were conveniently dismissed to live by their own wiles.

If you care to read a little about the treatment of these animals,
the writings of Carbonear's Philip Toque (1814–1899) are recom-
mended. In *Wandering Thoughts and Solitary Hours*, written in 1846,
he describes much horrific abuse of various animals:

> No animal in Newfoundland is a greater sufferer from man
> than the dog. This animal is employed during the winter

season in drawing timber from the woods, and he supplies
the place of a horse in the performance of several duties. I
have frequently seen one of these noble creatures drawing
three seals (about one hundred and thirty pounds' weight) for
a distance of four miles over huge rugged masses of ice, safe
to land...

I well remember seeing some boys taking a poor dog to
drown him. It is almost general practice in Newfoundland,
that after the poor animal has faithfully served his master,
and is no longer able to draw wood, there is a large stone
sufficient to sink him, fastened firmly round his neck, and
he is then thrown into the sea to die. The boys were engaged
in this most cruel and unfeeling practice when I saw them,
but in this instance instead of taking him to the sea, where
there was deep water, they were endeavouring to drown him
in a brook with hardly sufficient water to cover the poor
animal. The owner of the dog was looking on, and appeared
pleased...I remonstrated with him...He said, "I never before
heard that it was sinful to drown a dumb animal; if I had
thought so I am very sure I should never have done it."

I replied, "Cruelty to animals is a sin very little thought
of. It is certainly a transgression of God's law...A merciful
man...will be attentive to provide for the wants of those
animals that contribute to his pleasure and advantage; not to
overload and work them beyond their strength; not to drown
them when old, nor to beat or unmercifully injure them in
any way."

He said, "I am sorry I never thought of this subject before,
for I have drowned many dogs during my life; we will if you

please, go and rescue the dog from the hands of the children."

We found the poor dog nearly choked from the pressure of the rope around his neck, to which the stone was attached, in order to sink him when thrown into the water. After cutting off the rope, I was glad to find he was still able to walk, the boys had been endeavouring to drown him for nearly half an hour. It is now nearly four years since this occurrence took place, and the dog was living the last time I was at Carbonear, although not able to draw wood in the winter season; and the person who owned him exceedingly regretted that he should have ever been the cause of taking the life of an animal.

—Tocque,
Wandering Thoughts and Solitary Hours by Still Waters

Things hadn't changed much by 1854 when eminent British naturalist Sir William Jardine noted in *The Naturalist's Library* how horrified English visitors were by the treatment of these dogs. About the same time William Youatt, in his book *The Dog*, asserted that the dogs were forced to haul loads too heavy for them, beaten to encourage or to discipline them, and fed—if they were fed at all—only rotted fish. Half-starved and overworked, many died during the winter, and if they were fortunate enough to survive, the desperate and often diseased dogs were forced to hunt for a living, sometimes preying on livestock. If they lived through the summer, they were again put to work when winter returned.

Some of today's owners and breeders have not advanced much beyond the level of these early boors and should be treated as the criminals they are. These few are the chief reason Newfoundland rescue organizations remain in business. Irresponsible breeders perform inadequate investigations into the character and abilities of prospective owners; if the dogs are lucky, they are rescued from those who have proven themselves incompetent as dog owners. If they are unlucky, they suffer and die early.

Many of these unfortunates are chained outside, unfed and without water, neglected, and away from the company they require. Worse, many are also physically abused. It's difficult to overestimate the human capacity for cruelty. Often someone will acquire a Newfoundland and neglect to train it properly. When it grows to 150 pounds, and becomes unmanageable, the cowardly owner will chain up, neglect, or abandon it.

At the other end of the spectrum, there are those who care. The Newfoundland's best friend, Lloyd Nelson, runs Canadian Newf Rescue and has saved about thirty abused or neglected dogs each year since 1995. When Nelson places a dog with a new owner, he personally checks to ensure that they will not be neglectful or have children who might mistreat their new dog. One test he administers to determine whether someone may be a suitable owner is the "drool test." He carries a dog biscuit in his pocket; when he puts his hand near it, the salivating begins. He claims that "when the dog's drool flies everywhere," he soon finds out who should or should not have a Newfoundland.

Monica Dominguez of Spain was working in Germany when she encountered her first Newfoundland. She became so enamoured of the breed that she immigrated to Newfoundland to be near the dogs and their place of origin. Now a breeder, she has become intensely involved, along with Jackie Petrie of Flat Rock, with Canadian Newf Rescue. Manitoba's Terry-Ann Lambert is another angel of hope for these dogs.

Anyone contemplating getting a Newfoundland dog as a pet should first check with a rescue association. If you really want a Newfoundland you will be able to find a dog who needs your help without much difficulty. The author's family has rescued four abused Newfoundlands, each of whom became valued and loving members of the household.

Sometimes these dogs have physical or psychological problems because of neglect or abuse, but these problems can be overcome. Adopting one can be a very rewarding experience; you will probably save a life and gain a great friend.

Glossary

Algonquin — Of or related to the First Nations living in eastern Ontario of Quebec.

banker — Vessel engaged in cod-fishing on the offshore grounds, esp the Grand Banks. A fisherman so engaged.

bedlamer — A young seal, especially a harp, approaching breeding age.

bent — A nautical term, meaning to tie or fasten a rope or line; as " a line was bent to…"

Beothuk — A nation, now extinct, that inhabited Newfoundland.

Biscayneer — Fisherman from the Basque area of France and Spain. Notorious in the latter half of the 1700s, Biscayneers were followers of a Spanish merchant from Tolosa who collected his men from around the Bay of Biscay. The word was used by way of reproach, they being little less than pirates, and from it is likely derived "buccaneer."

bogey — A small stove originally used on a fishing schooner; applied generally to any small coal- or wood-burning stove.

braw — A Scottish word meaning excellent, splendid, making a fine appearance.

breeches buoy	A ring lifebuoy suspended from a line that has canvas "breeches" for the user's legs. Contact is made with the shore using a rocket gun, a line is strung, and those in peril are pulled to safety along the line.
brewis	Sea biscuit or hardtack, soaked in water and boiled with codfish, pork fat, and vegetables.
capelin	A small iridescent deepwater fish, very similar to smelt.
clew-claws	Dew claws.
clog	Encumbrance or impediment; a block of wood to impede an animals movement; i.e. a clogged dog.
coaster	A vessel that trades along a coast.
cornet	The fifth commissioned officer in a cavalry troop, who carried the colours.
cracky	Small, noisy, mongrel dog.
cynophobia	Fear of dogs.
dew-claw	A rudimentary inner toe found on some dogs; the equivalent of a thumb.
droke	Small valley with steep sides, sometimes wooded and with a stream.
fathom	Nautical measure of depth equivalent to six feet.
fient	Scottish variation of fiend.
figgy-dowdy	Suet pudding with raisins.

fish flake	Not a Newfoundland breakfast food—see *flake*.
flake	Platform built on poles and spread with boughs for drying codfish near the beach.
flanker	A burning ember from a wood fire; a large spark.
flews	Pendulous lip, particularly that part at the "corners" of the mouth.
floater	The cod-fishery in Labrador waters prosecuted by migratory fishing schooners from Newfoundland; the crew lived on the vessel.
front	The leading edge of the ice that moves south in the spring and on which the seal herds whelp.
gybed	Of a sail, when it swings across in wearing or running before the wind.
harp	A breed of seal.
highliner	A ship or fisher that has the greatest catch.
ice claw	Grapnel attached to a line and used to anchor a vessel to the ice.
inshore	Near the shore.
jig	To fish using a jigger.
jigger	Weighted, unbaited hook or hooks used to catch cod.
jowler	A skilled and energetic sealer or fisher.
knot	A unit to measure the speed of a ship.
landwash	The seashore between high and low tide marks.

livyer	Permanent settler on the coast.
longer	Long pole used horizontally in constructing flakes, stages, roofs, etc.
lugs	Ears.
mamateek	Beothuk winter house.
mauzy	Of the weather; foggy, misty, damp.
Mi'kmaq	First Nations people living in the Maritimes.
outcross	The result of breeding animals not closely related.
outport	Newfoundland coastal settlement, other than St. John's.
pan	A flat piece of floating ice broken free from the general ice mass.
polynya	Stretch of open water surrounded by ice.
skiff	Small seagoing boat, adapted to rowing or sailing.
sou'wester	A waterproof hat with a broad brim, elongated and sloping at the back.
stage	Platform with sheds, working tables, etc., where fish are landed and processed and gear and supplies are stored.
stays	The moment when a tacking vessel is head to the wind; to put in stays.

sunker   Submerged rock over which the sea breaks.

swile, swoil   A seal; hence swiler or swoiler, sealer.

taffrail   After rail at the stern of a ship.

tern schooner   Three-masted schooner.

tickle   Narrow salt-water strait, between islands or other
                      land masses.

tilt   A temporary shelter usually constructed of logs set
                      vertically in the ground.

touten   Bread dough fried in fat.

trap-skiff   A large, undecked fishing boat propelled by oars,
                      small sail, or engine, used in the coastal fishery—usu-
                      ally to set and haul nets, especially cod traps.

water dog   Large, usually black, smooth-haired dog with webbed
                      feet; the original dogs of Newfoundland. They have
                      since evolved into two breeds, the Newfoundland dog
                      and the Labrador retriever.

whalpit   The Scottish variation of "whelp," here meaning a
                      young puppy.

Bibliography

Adler, Judi, and Ellis Adler. "Lindsey," on *Sweetbay Newfoundlands*, http://www.sweetbay.com/lindsey.htm (accessed September 8, 2005).

Adney, Tappan. *Tales of the Canadian North*. Secaucus, NJ: Book Sales, Castle, 1984.

American Kennel Club. "AKC Gazette: The Official Journal for the Sport of Purebred Dogs." http://www.akc.org/pubs/gazette/ (accessed September 8, 2005).

———. *The Complete Dog Book*, 16th ed. New York: Howell Book House, 1982.

Andrieux, J. P. *Shipwreck at St. Pierre*. Lincoln, Ont: W. F. Rannie, 1982.

The Atlantic Advocate. University of New Brunswick Press. October 1976.

Bardens, Dennis. *Psychic Animals*. New York: Henry Holt, 1988.

Bealby, J. T., and Ford Fairford. *Peeps at Many Lands, Canada and Newfoundland*. New York: MacMillan, 1921.

Booth Chern, Margaret. *The New Complete Newfoundland*. New York: Howell Book House, 1975.

Brown, Addison. *Newfoundland Journeys*. New York: Carlton Press, 1971.

Brown, Cassie E. "Hero is a Fake," in *Seadogs and Skipper*, edited by Garry Cranford. St. John's: Flanker Press, 2002.

Brown, Dave. "Brown's Beat," in *The Ottawa Citizen*, December 24, 1999.

Burin Senior Citizens Association. *History of Burin*. Marystown: South Coast Printers, 1977.

Chambers, Robert. *Book of Days*. Philadelphia: J. B. Lippincott, 1879.

Cock-a-Doodle-do! Father Tuck's Nursery Series. London: Raphael Tuck and Sons [1920?].

The Constitution (Cork, Ireland), September 18, 1849.

Cormack, W. E. *A Narrative of a Journey Across the Island of Newfoundland, 1822.* London: Longmans, Green, 1928.

Cranford, Gary, ed. *Not too Long Ago.* St. John's: Seniors' Resource Centre, 1999.

————. *Sea Dogs and Skippers.* St. John's: Flanker Press, 2001.

Cuff, Robert, author; and Derek Wilton, editor. *Juke's Excursions.* St. John's: Cuff Publications, 1993.

Cummins, Bryan. *Dogs in Canada.* Etobicoke: Apex Publishing, 2003.

Currey, John E. *Sailors and their Ships.* Garnish: J. E. Currey, 1999.

D'Aulaire, Emily and Per Ola. "The Bravest Dog," in *Reader's Digest,* December 1984.

Davidson, Keith. "Newfoundland Dogs Breed History," on the website

Dogs Annual. Etobicoke: Apex Publishing, 2002.

Dogs in Canada. Etobicoke: Apex Publishing, April 1999, April 2002, May 2003, July 2003, August 2003.

Dogs with Jobs, television program on the Life Network, June 2004 (Episode 42).

Downhome. "Dog Takes On Bear to Save Family," December 2000.

————. "Newfoundland Dog Saves Woman," June 1997.

————. Pride of Newfoundland and Labrador, June 1998.

Drury, Kitty, and Bill Linn. *Newfoundlands.* Neptune City, NJ: T. F. H. Publications, 1989.

Drury, (Mrs.) Maynard K., ed. *This is the Newfoundland.* 2nd ed. Newfoundland Club of America, October 1978.

Encyclopedia of Newfoundland and Labrador. Newfoundland Book Publishers, 1967.

Fitzgerald, Jack. *Newfoundland Fireside Stories*. St. John's: Creative Publishers, 1990.

Fox, Arthur. *The Newfoundland Constabulary*. St. John's: Robinson Blackmore, 1971.

Fraga, Brian. "The hairy heroes of search and rescue," in *The Herald* (New Britain, Connecticut), January 21, 2003.

Galgay, F., and M. McCarthy. *Buried Treasures of Newfoundland and Labrador*. St. John's: Harry Cuff Publications, 1989.

———. *Olde St. John's*. St. John's: Flanker Press, 2001.

———. *Shipwrecks of Newfoundland and Labrador*. St. John's: Creative Publishers, 1997.

Green, Pam. "Don't buy a Bouvier!" [paper]. c. 1992.

Hamer, Blythe. *Dogs at War: True Stories of Canine Courage under Fire*. London: Carlton Books, 2001.

Hamilton, W. R. *The Yukon Story*. Vancouver: Mitchell Press, 1964.

Hatton, Joseph, and Moses Harvey. *Newfoundland, the Oldest British Colony*. London: Chapman & Hall, 1883.

Hausman, Gerald, and Loretta Hausman. *Useless Facts and The Mythology of Dogs: Canine Legend and Lore through the Ages*. New York: St. Martin's Press, 1998.

Horwood, Andrew. "Dogs That Were No Fiction," in *Newfoundland Stories and Ballads*. Summer–Autumn 1969.

———. *Newfoundland Ships and Men*. St. John's: Macy's Publishing, 1971.

———. *Newfoundland*. Toronto: Macmillan, 1969.

Jesse, Edward. *Anecdotes of Dogs*. London: Richard Bentley, 1858.

Jukes, J. B. *Excursions in and About Newfoundland During the Years 1839 and 1840*. London: John Murray, 1842. Reprint, Toronto: Canadiana House, 1969.

Killilea, Marie. *With Love from Karen*. New York: Dell Publishing, 1963.

Kinsella, P. J. *Some Superstitions and Traditions of Newfoundland*. St. John's: MUN, Folklore and Language Publications, 1919.

Kirwin, W. J., G. M. Story, and P. O'Flaherty, editors. *Reminiscences of James P. Howley*. Toronto: Publications of the Champlain Society, 1997.

Kosloff, Joanna. *Newfoundlands*. Hauppauge, NY: Barron's Educational Series, 1996.

LaGow, Bette. "The Nanny," in *Dog Fancy Magazine*, August 1994.

Lumsden, James. *The Skipper Parson on the Bay and Barrens of Newfoundland*. Toronto: W. Briggs: 1906.

Lysaght, A. M. *Joseph Banks in Newfoundland and Labrador (1776); His Diary, Manuscripts and Collection*. Berkeley: University of California Press, 1971.

MacPherson, Harold. "Yesterday's Heroes." [documentary]. Produced by the Canadian Broadcasting Corporation.

———. "The Newfoundland Dog," in *The Book of Newfoundland*, vol. 1, edited by Joseph Smallwood. St. John's: Newfoundland Book Publishers, 1937.

Magner, D. *The Standard Horse and Stock Book*. c. 1903.

Marshall, Ingeborg C. L. *A History and Ethnography of the Beothuk*. Montreal: McGill-Queen's University Press, 1996.

Marshall, Logan, ed. *The Sinking of the Titanic and Great Sea Disasters*. New York: L. T. Myers, 1912.

McBurney, and Byers. *True Newfoundlanders*. Richmond Hill: Boston Mills Press, 1997.

McWhirter, Norris. *The Guiness Book of World Records*. New York: Bantam Books, 1983.

Menault, Ernest. *L'intelligence des animaux*. Paris: Hatchet, 1871. Reprint, 1890.

Millais, J. G. *Newfoundland and its Untrodden Ways*. London: Longmans, Green, 1907.

Morris, Edwin H. "The Newfoundland Dog," in *American Kennel Club Gazette,* January 31, 1925.d

Mosdell, H. M. *When Was That?* St. John's: Robinson Blackmore, 1974.

Mott, Maryann. "Guard Dogs: Newfoundlands' Lifesaving Past, Present." *National Geographic News*. 7 February 2003.

Mowat, Farley. *The New Founde Land*. Toronto: McClelland-Bantam, Seal Books, 1989.

Moyles, R. G. *Complaints is many and various, but the odd Divil likes it*. Toronto: Peter Martin, 1977.

Mullaly, John. *A Trip to Newfoundland*. New York: T. W. Stron, 1855.

Murphy, Michael P. *Pathways Through Yesterday*. St. John's: Town Crier Publishing, 1976.

Myers, L. T. *The Sinking of the Titanic and Great Sea Disasters*. New York: L. M. Myers, 1912.

The Naturalist's Library. Sir William Jardine. London: 1845.

Newfoundland Conventioneer and Tourism Guide. Vol. 12, no. 1, 2001.

Newfoundland Stories and Ballads. St. John's: Summer/Autumn, 1967.

New York Herald, October 23, 1849, and November 12, 1849.

Nutbeem, Megan. "The Newfoundland Dog". Typescript. August 26, 1988.

———. "The Newfoundland Dog." In *The Book of Newfoundland*, vol. 3., edited by Joseph Smallwood. Saint John: Newfoundland Book Publishers, 1967.

O'Flaherty, Patrick. *The Rock Observed*. Toronto: University of Toronto Press, 1979.

O'Neill, Paul. *Breakers—Stories from Newfoundland and Labrador*. St. John's: Breakwater Publishing, 1982.

Outing Magazine, February 1903: Children of the Bush. Secaucus, NJ: Book Sales, Castle, 1984.

Panama Herald, May 6, 1853.

Parker, John P. *Cape Breton Ships and Men*. UK: Hazel, Watson & Viney, 1967.

Parsons, Robert. *Committed to the Deep*. St. John's: Creative Publishers, 1999.

———. *Lost at Sea, a Compilation*. St. John's: Creative Publishers, 2002.

Pedley, Charles. *History of Newfoundland*. London: Longman, Green, Longman, Robert & Green, 1863.

Perlin, A. B. *The Story of Newfoundland*. St. John's: Perlin, 1959.

Peyton, Amy Louise. *River Lords: Father and Son*. St. John's: Jesperson Press, 1987.

Pickett, P., and Judy Ferguson. *Heroic Companion*. Grand Falls–Windsor: Robinson Blackmore, 2001.

Pierce, L., and D. Whitefield. *A Treasury of Prose and Verse Book 2*. Toronto: Ryerson Press, MacMillans in Canada, 1928.

Poe, Edgar Allan. *The Narrative of Arthur Gordon Pym*. 1838. Reprint, New York: Penguin Books, 1999.

Pratt, E. J. *Here the Tides Flow*. Toronto: MacMillan of Canada, 1962.

Prowse, D. W. *A History of Newfoundland*. London: Macmillan, 1895.

Puhr, Liz. "The rescue of Napoleon," from a website about Newfoundland breed history: http://www.mindspring.com/~atlnewf/newfl/history/napolean.html (accessed September 9, 2005).

Reader's Digest. *Reader's Digest Illustrated Book of Dogs*. 1993.

Reid, Dennis. *A Concise History of Canadian Painting*. Oxford University Press: London, 1973.

Ricketts, Bruce. "The SS *Ethie* and the Dog Collar," on *Mysteries of Canada*,. http://www.mysteriesofcanada.com/Newfoundland/Ethie. htm (no longer active at time of publicatio).

Roberts, Kenneth. *Trending into Maine*. Boston: Little, Brown, 1938.

Robinson, G., and D. Robinson. *The Nellie J. Banks*. Summerside: Alfa-Graphics, 1972.

Ryan, and Rossiter. *The Newfoundland Character*. St. John's: Jesperson Press, 1984.

San Francisco Bulletin, November 2, 1855.

Satkofsky, Amy. Article in the Pennsylvania *Express-Times*, February 13, 2003.

Savory, Lori. *Newfoundland Lifestyle*. St. John's: Communications 10, [date unknown].

Scott, George, and John Middleton. *The Labrador Dog*. London: H. F. & G. Withersby, 1937.

Scott, Sir Robert. *The Sportsman's Repository*. London: Sherwood, Neely, and Jones, 1820.

Smallwood, Joseph R. *The Newfoundland Character*. St. John's: Jesperson Press, 1984.

———. *The best of the Barrelman*. St. John's: Creative Publishers, 1998

———, ed. *The Book of Newfoundland*. 6 vols. St. John's: Newfoundland Book Publishers, 1937–1967.

Smith, J. Harry. *Newfoundland Holiday*. Toronto: Ryerson Press, 1952.

Thomas, Aaron. *The Newfoundland Journal of Aaron Thomas, 1794*. London: Longmans, Green, 1968.

Tocque, Philip. *Wandering Thoughts and Solitary Hours By Still Waters*. London: 1846.

————. *Newfoundland as it was and as it is in 1877*. Toronto: John B. Maguen, 1878.

Townsend, Charles W., ed. *Captain Cartwright and his Labrador Journal*. Boston: Dana Estes, 1911.

Wakeham, P. J. "The Amazing Story of a Newfoundland Dog Named 'Skipper,'" in *New-Land Magazine*. Saint Johns: 1990.

Walsh, Christian. "Community Hero: Mary Lou Naso and Harry," *My Hero,* http://myhero.com/myhero/hero.asp?hero=MaryLouNaso (accessed September 8, 2005).

Whitney, L. F., DVM. *The Complete book of Dog Care*. New York: Doubleday, 1985.

Willems Snopek, Roxanne. *Great Dog Stories*. Canmore, Alberta: Altitude Publishing Canada, 2003.

Wilson, William. *Newfoundland and its Missionaries*. Cambridge, Mass: Dakins & Metcalf, 1866.

Wix, Edward. *Outrageous Seas: shipwreck and survival in the waters off Newfoundland, 1583–1893*. Rainer K. Baehre, ed. Ottawa: McGill-Queens University Press, 1999.

Youatt, William. *The Dog*. London: 1845.

Young, Grant. "Wilderness and Water," in *Downhome*, October and November 199